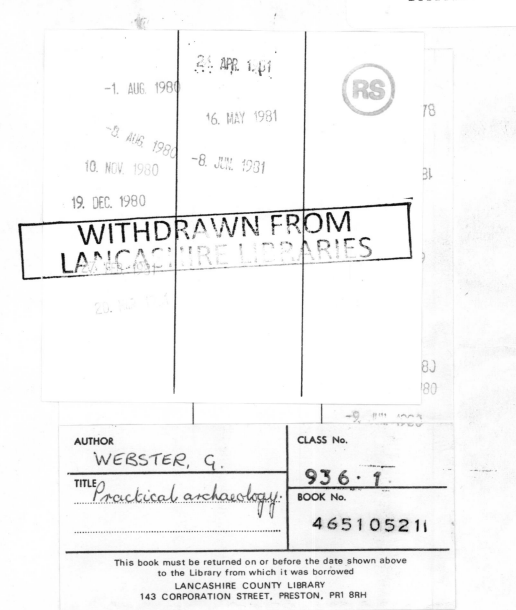

PRACTICAL ARCHAEOLOGY

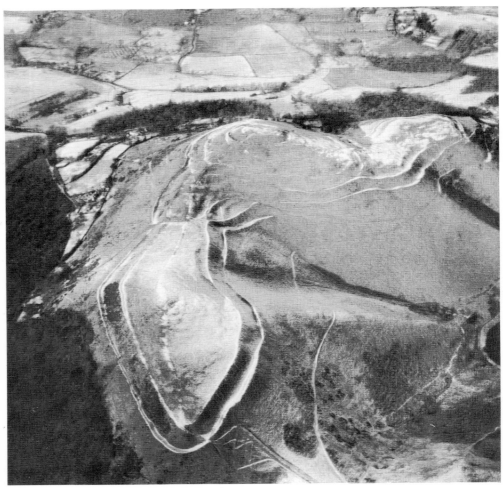

I   An air photograph of the Herefordshire Beacon.

GRAHAM WEBSTER

PRACTICAL ARCHAEOLOGY

An Introduction to
Archaeological Field-Work
and Excavation

WITH 11 PHOTOGRAPHS
AND 22 LINE ILLUSTRATIONS

ADAM & CHARLES BLACK · LONDON

FIRST PUBLISHED 1963
REPRINTED WITH MINOR CORRECTIONS 1965
SECOND EDITION (ENTIRELY RESET) 1974

A. AND C. BLACK LTD.
4, 5 AND 6 SOHO SQUARE, LONDON W1V 6AD

© GRAHAM WEBSTER 1963, 1974

ISBN 0 7136 1179 0

To
I. A. R.
For His Constant Help and Encouragement

465105211

FILMSET AND PRINTED IN GREAT BRITAIN BY
BAS PRINTERS LIMITED, WALLOP, HAMPSHIRE

Contents

Illustrations

Foreword to the first edition

This book is intended to be a companion volume to *Approach to Archaeology* by Stuart Piggott which sets out the basic ideas behind the subject. The present volume deals with the practical aspects and introduces some of the basic techniques developed by archaeologists to help them towards the solution of their problems in the field. These purely practical considerations are difficult to assimilate without contact with field realities, and students must realise that they cannot begin the process of mastering excavation methods until they put a spade into the ground. Once this start has been made much of this book will be read with a deeper understanding.

Had this book been written by a prehistorian the contents would have been quite different, with an emphasis on problems of chronology and tracing the movement and diffusion of cultures through potsherds and metal tools. Many of the kind of questions put by the prehistorian can be answered for Roman Britain by direct reference to the works of Roman historians or surviving inscriptions. As one who has spent much of his working life on the problem of the Roman occupation of Britain, I have drawn attention mainly to the problems of structures and stratigraphy. To some extent this and its companion volume complement each other.

As the student widens his experience by working on sites of different types and periods, he will become aware of the divergent views concerning the basic techniques of the archaeologist. The student should find by experience the type of work which appeals to him most, rather than attempt to specialise before sampling a few varieties. The excavator must learn to deal effectively with remains of all the periods he may encounter. His main object may be the investigation of a Roman villa, but he may find an eighteenth-century ice house or a medieval house above it and a Bronze

Age burial below and all these structures should be considered with equal care and devotion to the truth.

This book is designed mainly for the amateur who may find in archaeology a satisfying interest, providing he or she is willing to spend time and energy in learning the techniques and acquiring sufficient background knowledge. Britain is unusual in providing many opportunities for amateurs, and as their competence has developed, it has been possible for original contributions to knowledge to be made. There are now many ways in which the amateur can learn by attending training schools and adding to experience by assisting in excavations where voluntary assistance is welcomed. There is great scope throughout Britain for the amateur to play an effective part, and competent observers are needed everywhere to check the flood of evidence being lost in ploughing, building developments and mineral workings.

If this book helps the beginner in his first steps towards an understanding of archaeological field methods so that he or she can the more readily make effective contributions, it will have achieved its main purpose.

I am greatly indebted to Professor I. A. Richmond and Mr A. L. F. Rivet who read chapters 3 and 2 respectively and made suggestions for adding to and improving the text which have been incorporated; also to my brother-in-law Mr Frederick Reed and Miss Christine Johnson who in the capacities of *advocati diaboli* have removed many minor errors and ambiguities. Many of the illustrations are the admirable work of Mr Brian Hobley who has especially placed me in his debt.

I am also grateful to Mr Martin Biddle and Professor S. S. Frere and the Society of Antiquaries for permission to reproduce Plates 5 and 7 and Fig. 13; to Mr Arnold Baker for his aerial photographs; to Mr Philip Rahtz for his photographs of Cheddar, to Dr Martin Aitken for his photograph of the gradiometer and to Mrs Muriel Stanley for compiling the index.

Foreword to the second edition

In the eleven years which have passed since the first edition of this book, great changes have taken place in both the field techniques and attitudes towards archaeology in Britain. This is due largely to the large scale emergency excavations made necessary by development with the considerable financial backing of the Department of the Environment. The directors engaged on these difficult operations have been forced by circumstances to develop methods of working with maximum efficiency sometimes at great speed to extract as much as possible from the ground before the site is destroyed. My book was then, and still is, based on the assumption that the excavator has adequate time to carry out his work. A modest-sized Roman villa may take up to twenty-five years in three to four week seasons and this is in striking contrast to the 43 days in which the research group of the Council of Kentish Archaeology stripped a building 200 ft by 50 ft (part of the Darenth Villa, *Current Archaeology*, 19 (1970), 221). We hope that one of these skilled directors will eventually produce a manual for archaeologists working under these pressures. My book has always been intended for the amateur operating in a very modest way and in spite of the changing attitudes there is still happily a place for the small groups helping on the large-scale emergencies or working on their local sites, providing always they have competent leaders and submit themselves to the rigorous discipline and the high standards demanded of modern excavation techniques.

Another factor in the digging scene is the growing application of scientific methods in the field and laboratory with which it is difficult to keep abreast and I have endeavoured to bring this edition up to date in this respect. The greatest changes are in chapter III. In 1963, I had begun to realise that the system of excavating in the system of grids was becoming rapidly out of date, but both this method and that of open stripping were described. Now the latter has completely superseded the old grid method except for the limited trial investigation. But the new system, still in an early stage of development, is very difficult to describe and presents many technical problems. I am most grateful to my colleagues, Mr Martin Biddle, Mr Philip Rahtz, Mr Donald Mackreth and Mr Philip Barker for being so patient and giving up so much time in discussing these new methods with me. I am grateful to the many others who have helped by indicating mistakes and inconsistencies which I have tried to eliminate but so much has been rewritten that doubtless more errors have crept in and I must take full responsibility for them.

Trying to bring this book into the new and rapidly developing situation is like pouring the proverbial new wine into an old bottle. It might have been far better to have scrapped it and started afresh, but this has not been possible, so I hope that for the beginner it may be a useful introduction.

Abbreviations used

Ag. Hist. Rev.	*Agricultural History Review*
Antiq. J.	*Antiquaries Journal* published by the Society of Antiquaries, London
Archaeol. Aeliana	*Archaeologia Aeliana* published by the Society of Antiquaries, Newcastle-upon-Tyne
Archaeol. Cambrensis	*Archaeologia Cambrensis* published by the Cambrian Association
Archaeol. J.	*Archaeological Journal* published by the Royal Archaeological Institute
Archaeol. N.L.	*Archaeological News Letter*
BM	British Museum
Bull. Board Celtic Stud.	*Bulletin of the Board of Celtic Studies*
Bull. Inst. of Archaeol.	*Bulletin of the Institute of Archaeology*
C14	Carbon 14
CBA	Council for British Archaeology
English Hist. Rev.	*English Historical Review*
Flints Hist. Soc. Publ.	*Flintshire Historical Society Publications*
Geogr. J.	*Geographic Journal*
Hants Fld Club & Archaeol. Soc.	*Hampshire Field Club and Archaeological Society*
HMSO	Her Majesty's Stationery Office
Ibid.	*Ibidem,* the same
J. Roman Stud.	*Journal of Roman Studies* published by the Society for the Promotion of Roman Studies

Medieval Archaeol.	*Medieval Archaeology* published by the Society for Medieval Archaeology
Norfolk Archaeol.	*Norfolk Archaeology* published by the Norfolk and Norwich Archaeological Society
OS	Ordnance Survey
pva	polyvinyl acetate
Proc. Dorset Natur. Hist. & Archaeol. Soc.	*Proceedings of the Dorset Natural History and Archaeological Society*
Proc. Prehist. Soc.	*Proceedings of the Prehistoric Society*
Proc. Soc. Antiq. Scot.	*Proceedings of the Society of Antiquaries of Scotland*
Proc. Somerset Archaeol. & Natur. Hist. Soc.	*Proceedings of the Somerset Archaeological and Natural History Society*
RCHM	Royal Commission on Historical Monuments
Trans. Birmingham Archaeol. Soc.	*Transactions of the Birmingham Archaeological Society*
Trans. Bristol & Glos Archaeol. Soc.	*Transactions of the Bristol and Gloucestershire Archaeological Society*
Trans. Essex Archaeol. Soc.	*Essex Archaeological Society Transactions*
VCH	*Victoria County History*
Wilts Archaeol. & Natur. Hist. Mag.	*Wiltshire Archaeological and Natural History Magazine*
Yorks Archaeol. J.	*Yorkshire Archaeological Journal*

1. Archaeological organisation and publications in Britain

Introduction

Archaeology is strictly concerned with the study of the material remains left by Man, but this study ought never to exclude Man himself. One can sometimes become so engrossed in pieces of worked stone or potsherds that the people who made and used them tend to be forgotten. It is a critical moment when the archaeologist ceases to think about the people he is investigating and begins to concentrate solely on their artifacts, for at this point his studies detach themselves from reality. Cultures in the remote past can often only be approached through a very small number of imperishable objects which happen to have survived. Of the peoples themselves, their ideas and institutions, there is no indication except for their faint reflections in primitive societies living in similar conditions in different parts of the world today.

It is the archaeologist's task to attempt a reconstruction of the Past in all its aspects, drawing on all the evidence he can obtain by finds and implication. The task can never be completed, since the reconstruction cannot be brought to a final conclusion. This must never prevent the attempt, for in moving forward hopefully one begins to arrive at a rather shadowy appreciation of the truth, and with further efforts the outlines may strengthen and blank areas begin to take shape.

Archaeological literature for popular taste inevitably dwells on the more exciting discoveries, usually with a wealth of objects in precious metals, of fine craftsmanship or of artistic merit. Such survivals from antiquity, usually from graves, are of great importance in appraising the wealth of early peoples and their technical skill or trading connections, but no matter how much they fascinate by their very strangeness, their importance should not be exaggerated: in the case of exotics, for example, they are totally alien to the cultural context in which they are found. It was Pitt-Rivers who recognised the value of ordinary things in bringing a greater understanding of everyday life through the study of pots, tools and articles of clothing as well as the homes. It is unusual for amateur workers in Britain to find objects of outstanding interest or beauty; normal discoveries consist of potsherds and humble scraps of ironmongery and a few pieces of bronze. The real importance of these fragments is not often in themselves as objects of interest but the possibility they have by their shape or method of manufacture of assessing their date. This helps to date the deposit or layer in which they are found. What is crucial here is the precise relationship between dateable artifacts and their position in the archaeological stratification. The beginner has a natural thrill in finding these objects, but soon he must begin to appreciate the greater significance of structures and their associated deposits. One of the most unfortunate factors in British archaeology recently has been the advent of the treasure hunters with their metal detectors. They often hunt in packs like hungry wolves stripping metal finds from the surface and even digging holes in pursuit of their quarry. The object of this activity is not the addition of knowledge but to sell anything of intrinsic value. Once an object is removed from its context and the information lost its archaeological value is nil. There is at present no satisfactory legislation to prevent this destructive activity.

Once a spade is put into the ground the excavator should feel committed to a total study of the site, giving equal weight to all periods and assessing in as precise terms as possible the complete history of the occupation and the types of buildings and people who lived and worked there. To accomplish this it is necessary to have a sound background knowledge of the periods likely to be encountered on the site. A serious fault in many amateur excavators is a lack of this, and their consequent inability to see their site as anything but a purely local matter. Almost all occupation sites and monuments of antiquity are part of a pattern, sometimes on a regional, sometimes on a national, and sometimes on a continental scale. The shifting and overlapping cultures with which they are associated need to be studied in the widest relevant context. The local amateur must at times lift his eyes beyond the close confines of his site or locality. If he is prepared to submit to the disciplines of field research, he ought also to accept the need for extensive reading and study to give him a background against which his discoveries can have meaning and place.

The County Societies

For many years the vertebrae of British archaeology have been the county societies, some of which have been in existence for over a hundred years. Almost every English county, and many of those of Scotland and Wales, has its archaeological society, often combined with history and natural history. The keen amateur is well advised to join one of these bodies and take part in the winter meetings, summer excursions and other activities. The interests of all these societies vary; some have a judicious mixture, others favour the study of church and secular architecture. Field archaeology may play a small part in the programme owing to the small number of active participants, but it is usually considered with sympathy by the other members and funds may be available as well as the important provision of space in the society's transactions.

The publishing of an annual transactions or journal is one of the most important functions of the society and some have been doing it for a century or more. These volumes may vary considerably in quality, but in the mass they form a formidable library of British archaeology. County bodies, supported almost entirely by their members' subscriptions, still provide the main publishing vehicle for discoveries and reports on field-work and excavations which may not be of national significance. Unfortunately many of these societies are finding themselves in financial difficulties. This is due to the considerable rise in printing costs and the natural reluctance to increase the annual subscription to keep pace. At the same time there is a demand for higher standards, especially in illustrations, and for more space as more discoveries are coming to light which need to be published.

The county societies had at one time wealthy and influential patrons who gave them weight in social and political circles. The great changes in the structure of society during the course of this century have naturally had their effect; the people of wealth and power today seem to have little interest in antiquarian matters and the position of the societies has in this respect weakened. There has also been the growth of professionalism with the creation of new posts in State services, museums and the universities. Whereas at the beginning of the century the professional archaeologists could be numbered in ones and twos in this country, there is today a considerable corps employed by such bodies as the Department of the Environment, The Royal Commissions, the Ordnance Survey and the national and provincial museums, in addition to the growing number of posts in the universities. Most of the professionals are active supporters of county societies and willing to give their time freely on excursions and lectures. Nevertheless, the amateur status in British archaeology has gradually retreated from its dominant position held early in this century and throughout the preceding ones. At present there is a reasonable balance of gifted amateurs and professionals with similar standards, and there has been a marked tendency for some of our best professionals to have been recruited from the amateur ranks. The situation is, however, changing rapidly as the scale of emergency work has increased. It is now possible to be continuously employed on excavations and this has created a small but growing body of young people who attach themselves to sites or directors throughout the year. Very few of them have received any training and some not even any post-school education. There is a strong case for the establishment of training centres and for making it necessary for anyone to complete approved courses before being accepted as site supervisors or directors.

The Council for British Archaeology

There is a national co-ordinating body, the Council for British Archaeology,[1] which attempts to deal with the serious problems of the preservation of antiquities, monuments and buildings of historical interest which now beset the country and other societies. The CBA was formed in 1945, replacing the Congress of Archaeological Societies, and its influence has gradually become established. The membership extends to almost all societies and includes many other bodies such as universities and museums. The Council acts as a watchdog and voice in matters of government policy affecting archaeological matters, and works to prevent the damage and destruction of monuments as well as being concerned with general co-ordination. Through the Regional Groups, which function over most of the country, there is a forum where bodies of all kinds can meet and discuss problems of mutual interest. Here the representatives of the senior county societies can meet those of the younger element from the active field groups.

The CBA has other important functions, one of which is providing financial aid for publication. An annual sum is received from Government sources through the British Academy, and any society can apply for and receive a contribution towards the publication of a paper which is considered of sufficient merit and containing material of more than local interest. The total sum is very modest and does not go very far when spread out over all the applications, but at least in these difficult days it is a small help towards maintaining the country societies' transactions. Financial

[1] Address: 8 St Andrew's Place, Regents Park, London N.W.1.

help is also available to research groups and societies through the generosity of the Carnegie United Kingdom Trust and operated through the CBA. Applications can be made for help towards the purchase of equipment for excavating and surveying and other expenses provided a reasonable project is envisaged and that during the course of the work training facilities are given to members of the group. Another of the CBA services enables a subscriber to purchase individual offprints from many of the transactions of national and county societies normally available to members only. Thus one can maintain a library of material on subjects of special interest for a very modest outlay. There is also the Annual Bibliography (*Archaeological Bibliography for Great Britain and Ireland*), an indispensable volume for serious students since it contains complete details of all material published during the year, classified under author, county, period and subject. This series starts with 1940 and is especially valuable for collecting information about special subjects and material and also for compiling and checking references. Since 1968 the CBA has been publishing annually *British Archaeological Abstracts,* consisting of brief accounts of selected articles and reports. For the general amateur with no specialist bent or research task there is the *Calendar of Excavations* issued monthly to subscribers during the spring and summer and giving a list of all excavations where volunteer and paid help is needed. This enables the student to plan his spare time and holidays in advance with due regard for the type of site, its situation and the director.

The rôle of the amateur

Nor can it be said that the days of the amateur are numbered, for there has been a fresh impetus since the war due to a variety of factors. There is no doubt as to the general popularity of archaeology, stimulated by television programmes and maintained by a spate of books, many of excellent quality. Apart from the growth of interest by the general public, there has been an increase in the numbers of serious students taking up the subject as a hobby. As a spare-time occupation archaeology has much to offer: fresh air and exercise to the sedentary worker cooped up overlong in the office block or factory, the comradeship engendered in working with kindred spirits, and the joy of discovery. Young scientists in particular take readily to archaeology with its new and different type of challenge, both physical and mental. In an excavation there is work for everyone, from sheer navvying to delicate trowel and brush work, as well as washing pottery, surveying, drawing, photography and recording.

The new trend can be seen in the demand for training facilities. Excavation schools in the summer vacations organised by extramural departments for adult students were first started by the University of Newcastle-upon-Tyne at Corbridge, followed by the University of Nottingham at Great Casterton, Rutland; later they were developed by the University of Birmingham at Wroxeter near Shrewsbury. Others have followed with similar schemes, so that on most excavations in Britain today there is usually a nucleus of trained and experienced amateurs as well as beginners working under professional direction. Unfortunately in the last decade the position has changed again. The ease with which untrained people can get paid for excavating has reduced the demand for training and some of these schools are in a state of serious decline. At the same time some directors on emergency works have advertised training courses which vary greatly in quality. There are at present no established standards or accepted practices in teaching methods. It is unfortunate that some directors of excavations are not only untrained in methods but incapable of organising and writing a report for publication.

There are several types of excavation work open to the amateur. The training schools offer a programme of lectures and demonstrations based on an excavation, but the main object is that of training the student in the basic techniques rather than pursuing archaeological problems. On training excavations, on the other hand, the facilities for specialised training are there for those who need them, but the excavation takes first place. The benefits a student will receive from this arrangement depend on the director and his staff and the time that might be available. Almost all excavations are those now designated as rescue or emergency. They are the result of the many kinds of development such as motorways, housing schemes, factories etc which destroy all remains at or below ground level. With careful advance planning and collaboration with planners and developers, it is possible to be able to have time in which to carry out extensive and detailed excavations, providing one can have access to the sites. But this can be done only if the presence of the site can be determined in advance with some indication of its size and significance. There are still far too many sites which are vanishing without a trace because their presence was not suspected and no one was around when there may have been a possibility of their being seen when the ground was disturbed. This reflects the pressing need for more field work so that sites are recorded on maps and so are considered when development or new works are being planned. These excavations are largely financed by the Department of the Environment with local support, and some of them are on a very large scale involving many areas of detailed investigation over a period of years.

All this has tended to sharpen the distinction between the amateur and professional. While the former are usually members of local societies and groups, the latter are individuals with no loyalties to anyone beyond the work in hand.

Every year in Britain there are for the amateur excavator ample opportunities for experience over a wide range of sites and periods. In spite of this, it is noticeable that many students become attached to particular sites and prefer to dig there year after year rather than go elsewhere. They take great interest watching a site develop and getting to know it in detail as well as the joy of meeting old friends every year.

However, experienced amateurs are badly needed in their own areas to work on sites at weekends and in the long evenings. Continuous work of this kind cannot be found over the whole of the country but, by persistent enquiry, the serious amateur may be able to link up and develop, at a site not too far distant from his home, the experience gained on holiday.

The beginner may sometimes find that in his area there is a shortage of professional or good amateur leadership and therefore little opportunity for archaeological work. In this case an approach could be made to the local extramural department, or to the local museum to find out which societies organise meetings and hold winter classes. Local problems can then be investigated and experienced advice given when needed. With the CBA and its regional organisation on the one hand and the education authorities on the other, there is the possibility of fruitful collaboration.

It should be clear from this that there is no longer any need for the amateur to work in isolation. Indeed it would be dangerous for him to do so as it often leads to wasted endeavour and a superficial interpretation of the results. With the increase of specialisation in all fields, it is necessary even for professionals to seek advice and help in many directions, and it is all the more needful for the beginner to link up with an organisation which will bring help to bear on his immediate problems. There are here and there eager individuals and small groups actively excavating without much appreciation of what they are doing. The thrill of finding pieces of pottery, coins and small objects is sufficient in itself to keep them happy and satisfied. Little attempt is made to consider the context of their discoveries on either a local or regional scale, and least of all to publish the results. Their isolation also tends to make these people impervious to outside help and advice. The unfortunate result is that instead of making a contribution to the body of knowledge of the past, their misdirected zeal often destroys possible clues which might be of value to a more informed investigator.

One does not need to be a professional in order to make a useful or significant contribution. Indeed, British archaeology depends still for much of its research on the amateur. There is a greater need than ever for the watchful observer in these times of rapid erosion of so much of our country-side by building developments, afforestation and agricultural improve-ments. There are not enough professional fieldworkers to cover the ground thoroughly and the local amateur can play a useful part in looking around areas being developed or quarried away and also in finding out about development plans in his area so that the ground can be surveyed well in advance of obliteration. To carry out this work with efficiency and autho-rity, he will need to submit himself to learning and training in archaeologi-cal investigation and above all keep in close touch with the Planning Authorities, so that new discoveries can quickly be put onto local maps. Archaeology is always producing something new and occasionally startling; one should be braced to stand the shocks of new discoveries or of being proved quite wrong. Because it is in this very fluid state, British archaeo-logy is an exciting science, attractive to the eager, young and intelligent minds now beginning to grapple with its problems.

Sources of Information

Before embarking on any piece of fieldwork or excavation, or any other kind of archaeological research on a particular area or site, it is advisable to examine the evidence of previous workers on the site and chance discoveries in that locality. One may not always agree with the opinions of earlier writers but any definite information about archaeological features observed by competent authorities is worthy of study. Some of these reports may take one back several centuries. William Stukeley (1687-1765), the great antiquary of the eighteenth century, had very strange notions about Avebury and Stonehenge and the rituals practised there, but his copious notes and drawings of these monuments have proved of inestimable value to those studying them today. Although many sites of early occupa-tion are now being discovered for the first time, there may well be records of earlier finds of coins or pottery made there before their full significance was appreciated. Although it is often a great labour to go through the earlier records, one can sometimes be saved from falling into serious error by doing so.

The great quantity of published material on British archaeology and difficulties in consulting it are sufficient to daunt the student setting out on his task. Only the libraries of our universities and larger cities contain a reasonable amount of this literature. Fortunately there are some short cuts in the form of summaries of published sources. The most important of these are the volumes of the *Victoria County History* and the Royal Commission on Historical Monuments. The great *VCH* series was started with high hopes at the beginning of this century but was not completed; more recently, however, the work has been taken over by the Institute of Historical Research, University of London, and the series now continues. The archaeological summaries mostly belong to the first two decades of the century and the Romano-British sections reached a high standard under Haverfield. The prehistoric sections were written before the great advances in this subject and have an outdated look. The original scheme was to include in the first volume of each county a survey of the geology and natural history followed by chapters on: 1. Early Man, 2. Romano-British remains, 3. Anglo-Saxon remains, and 4. Ancient Earthworks. In recent issues this has been changed and there is now an archaeological gazetteer published of Wiltshire and a whole volume devoted to the Romano-British remains of Essex (v, 1966).[1]

Although much of it has now been superseded, these massive volumes represent a very considerable body of work and also an indispensable source of information. The only counties for which there is no *VCH* volume are Cheshire, Northumberland, Middlesex and Westmorland. The county of Northumberland, however, is favoured with a great history of its own in fifteen volumes, published from 1893 to 1940 and containing, especially in the last volume, important archaeological material.[2]

---

[1] The following are the volumes issued with dates of publication and archaeological contents using the numbers given above for the four main subjects:

Bedford, i, 1904 (1, 3 and 4), ii, 1908 (2); Berks, i, 1906 (1-4); Bucks, i, 1905 (1 and 3), ii, 1908 (2 and 4); Cambs, i, 1938 (1 and 3), ii, 1948 (4); Cornwall, i, 1906 (1 and 3), Pt. 5, 1924 (2); Cumberland, i, 1901 (1 and pre-Norman remains); Derby, i, 1905 (1-4); Devon, i, 1906 (4); Durham, i, 1905 (1, 3 and 4); Essex, iii, 1963; Hants, i, 1900 (1-4); Hereford, i, 1908 (1-4); Herts, i, 1902 (1 and 3); ii, 1908 (4), iv, 1914 (Celtic and Romano-British remains); Hunts, i, 1926 (1-4); Kent, i, 1908 (1, 3 and 4), iii, 1932 (2); Lancs, i, 1906 (1 and 3), ii, 1908 (4); Leics, i, 1907 (1-4); Norfolk, i, 1901 (1-3); Notts, i, 1906 (1, 3 and 4); Northants, i, 1902 (1-3), ii, 1906 (4); Oxford, i, 1939 (1-3), ii, 1907 (4); Rutland, i, 1908 (1-4); Shrops, i, 1908 (1, 2 and 4); Somerset, i, 1906 (1-3), ii, 1911 (4); Staffs, i, 1908 (1-4); Suffolk, i, 1911 (1-4); Surrey, i, 1902 (1 and 3); iv, 1912 (2 and 4); Sussex, i, 1905 (1, 3 and 4); iii, 1935 (2); Warwicks, i, 1904 (1-4); Wilts, i, Pt. 1, 1957 (Archaeological Gazetteer), Pt. 2, 1955 (3); Worcs, i, 1901 (1-3), iv, 1924 (4); Yorks, i, 1907 (1), ii, 1912 (3 and 4).

It will be noted that in the cases of Cambs, Cumberland, Devon, Dorset, Durham, Glos, Lancs, Lincs, Notts, Wilts and Yorks, the Romano-British sections have not been published, but Haverfield's notes for them are in the library which bears his name at the Ashmolean Museum, Oxford, and can be consulted on application.

[2] *History of Northumberland*, vol. xv, includes the paper by I. A. Richmond, 'The Romans in Redesdale', 63-159.

The Royal Commission's surveys are also on a county basis, arranged in parishes, but are mainly descriptions of visible remains.[1] As with the *VCH* there is little comparison between some of the early volumes and the more recent ones. This is especially true of Wales, where the early nine volumes (1911-1925) are very sketchy when viewed in comparison with those of Anglesey (1937) and the three Caernarvonshire volumes (1956, 1960 and 1964). Counties previously compressed into a single volume are these days expanded into three or four, and special volumes have been devoted to cities such as Cambridge, Oxford and Roman York (1962). It is unfortunate for archaeologists that the prehistoric, Roman and early medieval monuments cannot be extracted and published separately, as the cost of the whole volume puts the purchase of the series as it is issued beyond the normal pocket.

One must add to these two remarkable series, which represent the starting point of most enquiries, several other works: *A Gazetteer of Roman Remains in E. Yorks* by M. Kitson Clark (1935), *Archaeology of the Cambridge Region* by Sir Cyril Fox (1923), and the County Archaeologies series published by Methuen, but the last of these are surveys of a very modest kind mainly for popular consumption and, as can be seen from the dates of publication,[2] rather old fashioned; the notable exception is the most recent, on Wessex (1958), and they do include gazetteers. The Ancient Peoples and Places by Thames and Hudson[3] includes excellent, well illustrated surveys and include bibliographies but no detailed gazetteers. Another series prepared mainly for schools is that of the Regional Archaeologies published by Cory, Adams and Mackay.[4]

One of the most important sources of information is the Ordnance Survey. Since the last war, the Archaeology Division has been considerably expanded and a serious attempt is now made to record accurately all visible antiquities on the various issues of maps. Another important function of

---

[1] The English counties so far published are as follows:
Bucks, 2 vols. (1912 and 1913); Cambs (West) (1968) (North-East) (1972); Dorset (West) (1952) (Central 2 vols.) (1971) (South-East 3 vols.) (1970); *Eburacum, Roman York* (1962); Essex, 4 vols. (1916, 1921, 22 and 33); Hereford, 3 vols. (1931, 32 and 34); Herts (1910); Hunts (1926); London, 5 vols. (1924, 25, *Roman London* 1928, 29 and 1930); Middlesex (1937); Westmorland (1936).

[2] Berks (1931); Somerset (1931); Kent (1930); Middlesex and London (1930); Surrey (1931); Cornwall and Scilly (1932) and Sussex (2nd edn 1953).

[3] This so far includes prehistoric Wessex (*Wessex before the Celts*, 1958), *East Anglia* (1960), Celtic Britain (1963), South-West England (1964) and South-East England (1970).

[4] They include *The Severn Basin, South Wales, North Wales, Yorkshire, South-West Scotland, Wessex* and *The Roman Frontiers of Britain*.

this body is the preparation and publication of special period maps. So far these include Dark Ages (1935), Monastic Britain (1950), Roman Britain, 3rd edition (1956) and Iron Age of Southern Britain (1962). These maps bring together a vast body of archaeological information, as it has been necessary to extract all published archaeological material on a parish basis and record it in a set of 6-inch maps and a card index, copies of both of which can be purchased. For detailed information about particular sites or the antiquities of selected areas, the student might start here. It is not possible at present for the Ordnance Survey to deal with detailed enquiries by correspondence, but if the serious student is able to visit the Survey offices at Southampton, facilities are available for the inspection of the set of maps and the copying out of the relevant information.

As maps form the basis of much archaeological work, the field-worker in particular should familiarise himself with the various issues and their uses. Three booklets by the Ordnance Survey[1] offer a good introduction, but only by constant use can one become thoroughly familiar with the value of the maps of different scales and appreciate how well Britain is served in this respect in comparison with the rest of the world.

Since 1938 the Ordnance Survey has based all its maps on the National Grid. This is of singular importance to all archaeologists since it enables a very accurate description of a find spot or site to be given without recourse to an elaborate verbal description. The National Grid is based on kilometre squares and the one inch to the mile maps are cross-gridded with these. Using this scale and sub-dividing the squares into tenths, one can fix a site to the nearest 100 metres (ie. 109·3 yards). This may be reasonable for a general reference to a site, but if one needs to be more accurate and give a find spot in a particular part of a field, it is necessary to use the six inch to the mile maps. This scale map is now so arranged that each map is five kilometres square. Once more the divisions are in kilometres but it is now possible with the help of scales printed at the edge of the map to measure down to ten metres. A fixed point with a reference as accurate as this would need to be stated in ten figures, five in each direction. An alternative is to use letters instead of the first two figures, as each 100 kilometre square has an alphabetic reference. The practice is for the first set of figures to be the

[1] *A description of small scale maps,* 1947 (ie. quarter, half and one inch to the mile); *A description of medium scale maps,* 1947 (ie. two and a half inch and six inches to the mile) and *A description of large scale maps,* 1947 (ie. 1/2,500 and 1/1,250). There is also the valuable *Gazetteer of Great Britain,* 1953, giving the position of all features named on the Ordnance Survey quarter-inch maps in terms of the National Grid.

east-westing reading and the second the north-southing.[1]

Another store house of information is the National Monuments Record,[2] a branch of the Royal Commission on Historical Monuments (England) and incorporating the National Buildings Record. The objective of this archive is to collect information about ancient sites and historic buildings. There is also a rapidly growing library of aerial photographs with an index based on the National Grid.

Periodicals

In reviewing the periodic archaeological publications one naturally starts with the national societies, the senior of which is the Society of Antiquaries of London. Although Fellowship is by invitation, it is possible for anyone to purchase the publications. The finest of all archaeological publications in Britain is undoubtedly *Archaeologia,* which appears at approximately yearly intervals. The first volume appeared in 1770 and volume 104 in 1973, and the cost of new volumes is at present seven pounds. These magnificent books contain fully illustrated monographs, many of considerable length and importance, but covering all aspects of antiquarian and archaeological research. Unfortunately there is a cumulative index for only the first fifty volumes. The *Antiquaries Journal*[3] has in it papers of smaller size, interim excavation reports and a valuable series of notes, book reviews and contents of periodical literature on a world-wide basis. Two parts are issued yearly and cost £3.50 each. This periodical started in 1921 and superseded the *Proceedings,* which date back to 1849 and contain a great deal of information of local discoveries. There are general indices to the first ten volumes of the *Antiquaries Journal* and the whole thirty-two volumes of the *Proceedings.* One of the most important functions of the Society is the series of Research Reports which contain some of the most important British excavations. Thirty of these have been issued and all but three are British.[4]

Another important national society is the Royal Archaeological Institute,

---

[1] See OS booklet: *A brief description of the National Grid and Reference System.*

[2] Fortress House, 23 Savile Row, London W1X 1AB.

[3] The *Antiquaries Journal* can be obtained direct from Oxford University Press, Press Road, Neasden, London NW10 0DD and *Archaeologia* from Bernard Quaritch, 5-8 Lower John Street, Golden Square, London W1R 4AU.

[4] A list is given at the back of each issue of the *Antiquaries Journal* giving the price and details of the availability of each report. They can be obtained from Thames and Hudson Ltd, 30-34 Bloomsbury Street, London WC1B 3QP.

not to be confused with the Institute of Archaeology of the University of London. The RAI publishes annually the *Archaeological Journal* containing papers of medium length covering the whole field of archaeology. The first volume was issued in 1846 and the volume for 1971 was no. 128. The earlier volumes are mainly confined to architectural and ecclesiastical subjects but the last thirty years has seen a definite swing towards archaeology and these fine volumes now contain reports and papers of prime importance. The subscription, at two pounds a year, is at present extremely good value,[1] as it also includes a lecture series in the winter and an annual summer meeting held in different parts of Britain and occasionally on the Continent.

The British Archaeological Association, another national body, was founded in 1843 and publishes an annual *Journal* of about the same size as each part of the *Antiquaries Journal* but the contents, although normally of high quality, tend to be antiquarian rather than archaeological. There are national bodies for Wales and Scotland, the Cambrian Association[2] and the Society of Antiquaries of Scotland[3] respectively, which publish annually *Archaeologia Cambrensis* and the *Proceedings of the Society of Antiquaries, Scotland*.

Several national bodies cater for needs of workers in particular fields. The Prehistoric Society,[4] which in 1935 superseded the Prehistoric Society for East Anglia which had been founded in 1908, publishes an annual *Proceedings*. For the student of classics and classical archaeology there is the Society for the Promotion of Roman Studies, which publishes annually the *Journal of Roman Studies* and for students of Roman Britain and the north-west provinces *Britannia* which includes a very valuable summary of Romano-British discoveries; the majority of the papers in the former are concerned with classical literature and history. The Society maintains a very fine library and a collection of lantern slides which can be borrowed

---

[1] Intending members need to be proposed and seconded by existing members, who should have personal knowledge of the candidate, and there is an entrance fee of one pound. Details from the Hon. Sec., Miss W. Phillips, 304 Addison House, Grove End Road, London NW8 9EL.

Membership Secretary, Mrs H. Noel Jerman, Dolforgan Gardens, Kerry, Montgomery SY16 4DN.

[3] General Secretary, c/o the National Museum of Antiquities, Queen Street, Edinburgh, from whom details should be obtained.

[4] Membership by election and the entrance fee is one pound and annual subscription three pounds. Details from the Hon. Sec., Dr Ian Langworth, Dept of Prehistoric and Romano-British Antiquities, British Museum, London WC1B 3DG.

by members.[1] The Society for Medieval Archaeology was founded in 1957, and publishes *Medieval Archaeology* annually, with papers and very full and well classified notes on excavations and discoveries of the previous year.[2] The Society for Post-Medieval Archaeology began publishing an annual journal *Post-Medieval Archaeology* in 1967.[3] An important general publication is the quarterly review of archaeology, *Antiquity,* which includes papers and notes on new discoveries from all over the world.[4] There is also, since 1969, *World Archaeology*[5] published three times a year by Routledge and Kegan Paul Ltd, which covers aspects of the subject, especially field techniques, from all parts of the world. Useful for British students and enthusiasts is the well-illustrated magazine *Current Archaeology,*[6] issued six times a year, often with pungent editorial comment.

Museums

One of the main sources of information is the local museum. Some of these, like Dorchester, in Dorset, were started by and are still the headquarters of the county society and house its library as well as its collections. In other cases however, the burden of upkeep has forced the society to hand over its collections to the local government authority. The conditions vary from town to town and area to area. Not all museums are archaeologically minded and there are still a few local authority committees which have a very narrow view of the duties of their curator, expecting him to sit at his desk all day long instead of going out occasionally to collect specimens and investigate their context. In cities like Bristol, Chester, Colchester, Coventry, Gloucester, Leicester, Lincoln and Norwich there is a strong tradition of archaeological work and the curators of these museums and their staffs have played a large part in the excavations and observation of building work which has led to a new understanding of the problems of their towns' histories. It is more difficult when there is a large adjacent rural area since some curators do not find it easy to move far beyond the

---

[1] The annual subscription is £8.25 for the two volumes and £4.50 for *Britannia*, but for student-associates £2.25. Details from the Secretary, 31-34 Gordon Square, London WC1.

[2] The annual subscription is three pounds, students under 25 £1.50. Details from the Secretary, c/o the British Museum, London WC1B 3DG.

[3] Annual subscription three pounds, details from the Secretary, City Museum and Art Gallery, Alexandra Road, Portsmouth, Hants.

[4] Obtainable from Heffers Printers Ltd., King's Hedges Road, Cambridge. Annual subscription £4.

[5] Annual subscription five pounds, Reading Road, Henley-on-Thames, Oxon.

[6] Obtainable from 9 Nassington Road, London NW3 2TX, annual subscription £1.50.

boundary of the local authority in which their museum is situated. This is understandable if the town and not the county has to pay for the upkeep of the museum. One of the serious difficulties of British local government is the lack of co-ordination between town and county authorities, and they have always been suspicious of each other's rights and privileges. Archaeology and natural history know no such divisions, and where a county has no museum of its own it ought to be prepared to contribute towards the principal town museums, so that members of the staff can collect material from beyond the town boundaries and study its context. There is often an understanding in these matters. Several County museums like Dorchester and Devizes play a useful role in their areas in field work and excavations. Others like Oxford, Warwick and Worcestershire have field officers on the staff, who have a policy of systematic field work and there is now a growing body of archaeologists in planning offices, but the appointment can be too low in the hierarchy to be effective. What is needed are small archaeological units in every county and large city to keep pace with development. Plans are being discussed by the Department of the Environment for the creation of Regional Units and if adopted may be the start of a national antiquities service.

Ideally, the museum ought to be the centre of all archaeological activity, providing not only working space, committee and lecture rooms, but study collections of local material. The portable objects found in the course of the work should automatically go into the collections. There should also be a laboratory where metal objects in a serious state of corrosion could be treated and preserved, and a scientific study done on specimens. Although some of these provisions can be made, cramped for space and lacking in funds though many of our museums are, it is in this last requirement that there is a serious gap. Laboratory staff need to be highly qualified and trained for this kind of work yet it is impossible for them to be fitted into the local government staffing structure; the post usually ranks as a technical assistant who would need to be paid less than the curator and his staff. Thus it reduces the scale of a technical assistant to the level of a junior clerk or office boy. A good scientist can command a salary of at least £3,000 a year in industry and it is hardly likely that he would accept a third of this to work in a museum laboratory and remain on the same grade for the rest of his life. In the present state of things there is little possibility of a technician moving into the curatorial grades. The difficulty is being partially resolved with the formation of regional laboratories, serving the museums of a large area. This is a very sound idea, but even with appointments on a much better salary scale there are at present very few competent people willing to take them.

The curators and staffs of the provincial museums of this country are a dedicated group of people normally prepared to do a great deal to help the genuine research student and serious amateur. Usually if one wishes to know anything about a site, this is where one turns at the outset. There may be in the collections pottery or other objects from the site or area in which interest has been roused. There may also be unpublished notes and almost certainly knowledge of some kind to lead the questioner towards his goal. One may learn, for example, of the existence of private collections and of other archaeologists who in the past have carried out field-work or excavations and who, if tactfully approached, might be able to produce further information.

Local histories are not always reliable but sometimes contain pieces of observation and more often hearsay which may have some value. Another source is the local newspaper, the back files of which may stretch back a hundred years or more. The task of going through these in a systematic manner can be truly formidable and the reader can easily be lured away into the fascinating byways of local lore and events. Entries may be very sparse but they do exist and may provide a good first-hand account of an early discovery. There may also be manuscript material in the form of diaries and jottings which the local archivist may possess or know about. Some of the eighteenth- and nineteenth-century antiquaries were prolific writers of daily notes and can be a rich mine of local information. Most of the Stukeley papers, for example, have been published by the Surtees Society (vols. 73, 76 and 80), but those of the Reverend Skinner, the Somerset parson, still remain in manuscript form in the British Museum. The archives may include some early maps and estate plans and these can be of great value in showing the state of the fields at a known date. A remarkable example of this is the early eighteenth-century map of Calstone Fields, Wiltshire, showing the strips with the names of their cultivators. Crawford published this map with an aerial photograph taken in 1924 on which the strips can still be seen, though much eroded by the plough.[1] These old maps often show boundaries and buildings which have long since disappeared without trace.

Even parish registers can occasionally be helpful, as in the case of the remarkable entry in the register for the parish of Rodmarton in Gloucestershire for the year 1630, quoted by Lysons. This read in its original Latin entry: 'Hoc anno in agris in loco Hocberry vocato, dum sulcos aratro

[1] *Wessex from the Air,* 1928, pls. xxviii and xxix.

ducunt, discooperta sunt tessellata pavimenta, tegulae quibus ferrei clavi infixi subrutae, nummi quoque aenei Antonini et Valentiniani Impp: Incolae mihi dixerunt, se aeneos et argenteos nummos saepius ibidem reperiisse, nescientes quid rei essent: a patribus autem audivisse, Rodmerton ab illo loco translatam olim ubi nunc est positam esse. Apparet autem stationem aliquam Romanorum ibidem aliquando fuisse.'[1] Lysons records the persistence of the local tradition that the church was originally built in this field and was removed one night by the Devil to its present position.

Equally important are the field-names given on most estate maps, and this brings us to a consideration of the value of place- and field-names. The English Place-Name Society began publishing its valuable county surveys in 1925.[2]

The *Introduction* to the Survey, Vol. 1, pt. i (1924), contains chapters on the various elements, Celtic, English, Scandinavian, French etc, and also one by Crawford on Place-Names and Archaeology (pp 143-164) which should be studied by all would-be field-workers. Crawford points out the significance of the *chester* element in places of Roman origin: although this is by no means infallible, it is always worth investigation. There are names indicating the presence of ruined buildings in the mocking tones of Rat's Castle, Spider's Castle etc. *Stodfold* means an enclosure for a stud of horses and may indicate areas walled or ditched at one time. The variants of

---

[1] *Archaeologia*, 18 (1807) 114. The entry reads in translation: 'In this year, while ploughing the fields of a place called Hocberry, a tessellated pavement was found together with roof tiles with their nails still adhering and bronze coins of the Emperors Antonius and Valentinian. The local residents told me that they often found bronze and silver coins in that same place, ignorant of their nature: and that the older inhabitants had said that Rodmerton had been moved from that place to its present position. It seems that at some time some station of the Romans was there.'

[2] Their volumes include: Bucks (1925); Beds and Hunts (1926); Worcs (1927); North Riding Yorks (1928); Sussex, pt i (1929), pt ii (1930); Devon, pt i (1931), pt ii (1932); Northants (1933); Surrey (1934); Essex (1935); Warks (1936); East Riding Yorks (1937); Herts (1938); Wilts (1939); Notts (1940); Middlesex (1942); Cambs (1943); Cumberland, pts i and ii (1950), pt iii (1952); Oxon, pt i (1953), pt ii (1954); Derby, pts i-iii (1959); West Riding Yorks, pts i-viii (1961-63); Glos, pts i-iv (1964-65); Westmorland, pts i and ii (1967), and field-names have been included on an increasing scale in recent years.

There are in addition to these publications useful books on other counties such as: E. Ekwall, *Place-Names of Lancs* (1922); W. W. Skeat, *Place-Names of Beds* (1906); W. W. Skeat, *Place-Names of Berks* (1911); W. W. Skeat, *Place-Names of Suffolk* (1913); H. Alexander, *Place-Names of Oxfordshire* (1912); A. T. Bowcock, *Place-Names of Shropshire* (1923); W. H. Doignan, *Notes on Staffs Place-Names* (1912), and the valuable two volumes of the Place-Name Society by A. H. Smith, *Place-Name Elements* (1956).

beorg as barrow, berrow and bury may indicate tumuli, but not always since small mounds may have other origins. In Gloucestershire and Herefordshire they are often referred to as *tumps*. Other sites needing some investigation are those named after the Devil since they may refer to buildings, standing stones or earthworks thought by the Saxon colonists to have been the work of the Devil. Field-names which often indicate a buried building are Castle, Church or Chapel Field. At some time in the past when the plough has hit some masonry, or stone-work has been visible, the locals could only think of it as a building such as these. They may of course have been right, but it is surprising how many Roman villas are found in fields so named.

Sites of ancient occupation with a surface scatter of pottery and tiles have given rise to names like the Devil's Kitchen, Crock Hill, Tile Hill, etc. In the south one finds the word *chisels* which normally means simply gravel (OE *cisel*) used for a tessellated pavement. Crawford drew attention to the Anglo-Saxon description *fagan flore*—coloured or variegated floor—from which the village of Fawler in Oxfordshire derives its name. A 'stony field' may mean precisely what it says, but in a clay or sand and gravel area clearly must refer to building rubble. Similarly 'garbage' and 'scrabbs' are names of fields containing Romano-British occupation near Stanton Harcourt. On the other hand the words *wall* and *weall* may not signify masonry but there are several other more likely origins (see Ekwall, *Dictionary of English Place-Names*). Most field-names have obvious meanings but the odd ones are always worth some thought and there has been little attempt to make a comprehensive detailed survey of any area. This is a task an amateur field-worker could very well undertake in a small selected area provided he does not start to speculate too freely on origins without an adequate philological background. Probably more nonsense has been published by earnest local antiquaries on place-names than on any other subject.

Many archaeologists maintain that useful information can often be picked up by sitting in little country pubs listening to the locals. This is no doubt a most enjoyable method of doing research but the tales one gets are very garbled. Accounts of local discoveries of an unusual character are handed down from one generation to another but the time scale is often telescoped in the process and what is said to have been 'in my father's day' may turn out to be much earlier. Occasionally, one may be fortunate in finding the man who actually made a find and he can perhaps take you to the exact spot, but more often local traditions and folk-lore provide little in the form of serious information. Folk memory in most cases does not extend more than a century or so except in a country like Scotland where clan feuds still seem to exist in some areas. In England there seems to be very little folk memory left of that major upheaval, the Civil War of the seventeenth century, or even of more recent events. Genuine folk memory and local tradition may now be difficult to separate since the introduction in recent decades of the taste for the old and quaint for commercial purposes. Examples of this are the Lincoln Imp, entirely a twentieth-century fabrication, and the ludicrous idea that Pontius Pilate was born in Scotland—the very house, it is said, can be pointed out. It is unfortunate that popular appetite for antiquities should be fed on such spurious material for the sake of selling a few tawdry souvenirs. The truth is always a complex matter, rarely seen with complete understanding, but all serious archaeologists should accept it as part of their duties to see that the public have presented to them at least some inkling of the realities of our island's wealth of history and antiquity. As G. M. Trevelyan once wrote, 'if historians neglect to educate the public, if they fail to interest it intelligently in the past, then all their historical learning is valueless except in so far as it educates themselves'.

2. Investigation by field-work, visual observation and type of site ; Methods of investigation ; Aerial reconnaissance ; Scientific prospecting

The two kinds of activity, field-work and excavation, although so closely interrelated, demand different approaches and training. Field-work is of equal if not greater importance of the two, yet there are far too few workers in this discipline. The excitement and prospect of immediate discovery in an excavation tend to lure most potential archaeologists, especially amateurs, in that direction. Another factor accounting for the small number of field-workers is the lack of training facilities. There are very few opportunities for the student to become trained in this very difficult art. Even the departments of archaeology in the universities have failed to include adequate provision. Rather better field training is often given to students in historical geography and surface geology. In these two fields one can at least be taught how to observe and record surface indications in relation to maps. Yet for the serious archaeological student the rewards of this kind of work are very great. There are still many features on our ancient sites which are there to be observed and understood. On most sites, that great field-worker O. G. S. Crawford could see in a few hours more than all the visitors in the past hundred years.[1]

What are the qualifications for the skilled field-worker? Whereas an excavation by its very nature has to be a group effort, field-work is often done by individuals covering considerable areas on foot. One needs

[1] A full bibliography of Crawford's writings is to be found in the volume of essays presented to him on his sixty-fifth birthday, *Aspects of Archaeology in Britain and Beyond,* edited by W. F. Grimes (1951). His early book, *Man and his Past* (1921), although in many respects now superseded, is still worth reading, and in his later work, *Archaeology in the Field* (1953), is distilled the results of his life's work; it is also redolent of Crawford's own, very individual personality.

therefore a good deal of stamina and patience, but above all a flair for observation, seeing and understanding the slightest of swellings and undulations on the ground. Technically he should be trained in several kinds of surveying, with and without instruments, and in making records; he should also have a considerable knowledge of geology and agrarian history, and most important, be able to read maps and plans as easily as a book.

Basically, the task of the field-worker is to study surface indications and try to interpret their origins. The majority of the hollows and bumps in our fields and commons are due to six kinds of activity: 1. surface geological deposition and erosion; 2. agriculture over the last two thousand years; 3. ancient or more recent habitation indicated by ruined or buried structures; 4. construction of boundaries; 5. industrial activity and mineral workings; 6. construction of communications.

Geological agencies

The main structure of our landscape has been formed by the varying types of geological formations softened by erosion and disguised by the clothing of vegetation. Only where areas of rock outcrop or where a river cuts through a gorge is one immediately aware of this stony skeleton beneath. Britain has a very complex geological structure. Whereas some countries are vast areas of the same kind of rock in horizontal layers, in the greater part of England the geological strata are inclined, and as one proceeds from the south-east towards the north-west one crosses many different kinds of outcrop proceeding from the younger to the older deposits. This has created the many delightful variations in the British countryside. To the west and north the harder, older rocks, more resistant to the hand of time, stand as our highland zones. But above much of the solid geology, as the rock formations are called, are much younger deposits, the results of the Ice Ages, the last important geological time division. The melting of the ice sheets produced enlarged rivers and lakes, changing the earlier watersheds. The movement of the ice sheets across the land surface caused much erosion, especially on the softer rocks, grinding them down to particles varying in size from coarse gravel to fine silt. All this material, as well as larger lumps of rock, was embodied in the ice, and when the water melted this detritus was carried away by the torrents, in some places to be dammed up to form lakes and in others to be swept along or slowed down according to the pace of the river. The deposits carried by these melting waters were separated out by the variations in the speed and force of the currents, and were dropped when the velocity was no longer great enough to support them. The finest material was carried the furthest and finally settled in a

21

lake bed or delta. Covering large areas of Britain are dumps of this glacial material. The fine silt has been consolidated into boulder clay like that over much of Suffolk and Norfolk, but there are also deposits of sand and gravel and often all exist together. These dumps are so recent in geological terms that in many places they are still features of the landscape and form the moraines and eskers which the practised eye can readily observe along the river valleys and edges of the original glacial lakes. A thorough under-standing of these geological processes, in particular the more recent ones, and a recognition of the resulting formations is thus essential to the field-worker.[1]

Agriculture

The landscape of the lowland zones in England is almost entirely the result of man's activities in cultivating the land. The fields, hedges, woods and spinneys have all been created as the land has been developed. Nowa-days farmers have much better equipment than formerly and with the help of government subsidies can remove trees and hedges and attack the marginal areas with bulldozers to bring every possible square yard into cultivation. The history of farming in the lowland areas is a fascinating study of a sporadic attack on open and natural countryside by a series of enclosure acts over the last few centuries. This has virtually obliterated the pattern of the medieval open field system. But before the Anglo-Saxon settlement there were even earlier systems belonging to the prehistoric and Roman periods. What opportunity is there for still recognising some of these earlier elements? Fortunately there are still traces in the areas which have escaped the intensive ploughing of succeeding centuries. On the chalk downlands of Southern England it is still possible to see something of the Celtic field pattern.[2] But with modern highly mechanised farming methods there is little left of this faint palimpsest, and much detailed field-

---

[1] A useful introduction to this study, known as geomorphology, is G. Dury, *The Face of the Earth* (Penguin, 1959). There are two sheets of maps showing the solid geology at ten inches to the mile, published by the Geological Survey of Great Britain in 1957. The divid-ing line is E-W, from the Lake District across to the Yorkshire coast just north of Scar-borough. There are in addition sheets at six inches to the mile of the Drift maps, ie. the glacial geology, but only parts of the country have so far been published, and the issue is not expected to be finished within the next fifty years. It may be possible to consult the notes prepared for sheets not yet published at the Geological Survey at the South Kensing-ton Museum.

[2] *Field Archaeology, Notes for Beginners*, published by the Ordnance Survey (HMSO, 3rd edn 1951), is a useful start and contains a comprehensive bibliography. For a more recent review see the CBA publication *Field Survey in British Archaeology*, 1972.

work is urgently necessary for recording these vestiges before they vanish entirely from the surface of the ground. Fortunately, as will be demonstrated below, destruction by the plough does not mean the complete removal of this evidence as some of it can still be recovered in the form of crop-marks.

Crawford was one of the first field-workers to make accurate observations of this kind but little had been done since his day, except in Sussex, until the Royal Commission of Historical Monuments started a comprehensive field survey in Dorset. The problems and difficulties of such work have been well set out by H. C. Bowen, a worthy successor to Crawford in this work, in his booklet *Ancient Fields* published in 1961 by the British Association, which is a notable addition to the modest number of text books on field-work.[1]

The various types of field are closely associated with the kind of plough in use and this has differed not only from period to period but also from one area to another. It is this complex pattern which makes it impossible to lay down any hard and fast rules for would-be field-workers. Prehistoric farming has differed not only from period to period but also from one area to another. It was, in the lowlands, restricted to the lighter subsoils such as sand and gravel deposits and the chalk downs. The tools available were very primitive and little more could be done than scratch the surface of the ground with digging sticks, hoes and similar hand tools. It is possible that a light type of wooden plough drawn by oxen was in use before the end of the Iron Age but this is difficult to prove.[2] The shapes of fields produced by this kind of garden agriculture were small square plots. In a stony country the rejected surface stones were thrown to one side to form heaps or built up into boundary walls. No technical improvements were possible until the use of iron, which did not reach Britain in any quantity until the second or third centuries BC. The tipping of a ploughshare with iron makes it into a much more serviceable and useful tool than having one made only of wood. Following the Roman invasion more efficient ploughs were introduced, with coulters to cut through the ground and mould boards to turn the sod. There were probably several different types of plough[3] available during the Roman

[1] H. C. Bowen and P. J. Fowler, 'The Archaeology of Fyfield and Overton Downs, Wilts'. *Wilts Archaeol. & Natur. Hist. Mag.,* lviii (1962), 98-115.

[2] Evidence has been advanced for ploughing below Bronze Age barrows (W. Glasbergen, *Barrow Excavations in the Eight Beatitudes* (1954), 176; *West Cornwall Field Club Proc.,* I (1955–1956), and doubtless more will be forthcoming.

[3] E. C. Curwen, *Plough and Pasture* (1946); F. C. Payne, 'The Plough in Ancient Britain', *Archaeol. J.,* 104 (1948), 82-III; W. H. Manning, 'The Plough in Roman Britain', *J. Roman Stud.,* liv (1964), 54–65.

period and they would be used for various types of ground. Our knowledge of the early field systems is confined to the downlands w ere their
traces have been preserved. But many other areas in the fertile valleys were
under cultivation and it is reasonable to assume that with the improved
ploughs the size of the fields would tend to increase. Some of the so-called
Celtic fields of rectangular shape, at times over an acre in extent, have been
ascribed to a later period. As the evidence of the extent of cultivation in the
Roman period accumulates it is becoming clear that most of the lighter
subsoils were under plough and probably marginal lands as well.

The development of iron production produced not only better ploughs
but other new and important tools such as scythes and axes which made the
task of clearance much simpler. The Romans also brought with them ideas
about large-scale farming and practicable drainage schemes. A marketing
organisation sprang into being with the creation of roads and towns. Iron
Age farmers had been content to produce enough for their own needs and
the tribute due to their overlords. Under Roman conditions it became possible to plan surpluses for the markets and amass monetary capital which
could be devoted to bringing more land under cultivation and improving
buildings and equipment.[1] The story of the countryside in Roman times
has yet to be worked out, but investigations have shown that the farms of
the first and second centuries were modest affairs. There was a great
expansion in the late third and early fourth centuries which produced the
fine villas whose large and magnificent mosaic pavements have always
aroused general interest whenever they have been uncovered.[2] There is
very little trace of this development now visible on the ground. There are
very few cases where it has been possible to recognise with certainty the
presence of a field system associated with a Roman villa[3] although there
are some hints in aerial photographs. A notable example is the two hundred
acre system at Barnsley Park near Cirencester. Yet about six hundred villa
sites are known, and careful field-work will eventually bring its reward.

In other parts of the Roman Empire there is evidence of the large-scale
land allotments of the *coloniae*, which are arranged on a grid system of
squares with sides measuring 20 *actus* (288,000 square Roman feet) for

[1] Some of these points are developed by A. L. F. Rivet, *Town and Country in Roman
Britain* (1958).
[2] Some of the basic problems are discussed in *The Roman Villa* in Britain, edited by A. L. F.
Rivet (1969).
[3] The attempt to trace continuity into Saxon times by H. P. R. Finberg, *Roman and Saxon
Withington* (University of Leicester, 1955), is not wholly convincing.

retired army veterans. Within these allotments the individual colonists would arrange field systems to suit their needs.[1] Although there were three *coloniae* for retired veterans in Britain, no system of centuriation, as the rigid field grid is called, has yet been satisfactorily proved.

The Anglo-Saxon colonisation was based on individual settlement by tribes or family groups which were self-sufficient and independent. It was almost a return to Iron Age conditions of production measured by the needs of the unit and the overlord. For several centuries the Celtic survivors and newcomers must have lived side by side, but pressure of population and the inability of the older inhabitants to adapt themselves to the new conditions gradually forced them to migrate or to become the slaves of the more independent Saxons.[2] Here and there it is still possible to trace on the ground the open fields system round the early medieval settlements. Another element which has survived in hilly country is the strip lynchet. This is a narrow terrace cut into a hill-side by the action of the plough. One-way ploughing which turned the sod in the downhill direction gradually accentuated the terrace effect. Lynchets survive because they were narrow strips often on steep slopes and are not likely to have been ploughed out in later centuries. The coming of the tractor has changed the picture and many are now vanishing. By their very nature lynchets represent the use of marginal land and must belong to periods of great land pressure when some farmers were forced out of the better arable land. No one observing the strips on the steep sides of the dry valleys of the Cotswolds near Bath, for example, would suppose that this form of cultivation was by choice if the broad level tops of the limestone plateau had been available. The kind of economic and other pressures is difficult to assess. It would also be a mistake to regard all these lynchets as ancient.

By far the commonest visible form of cultivation is the ridge (or rig) and furrow. This corrugated effect can be seen covering the greater part of the Midlands and many other areas of Britain. The ridges take many forms, some straight, some curved, some broad, some narrow. Their origins have been the source of much speculation and the problem is complicated, since

[1] Examples of this can be seen in aerial photographs by John Bradford, *Ancient Landscapes* (1957), chap. iv.

[2] Archaeological evidence for Celtic survival in England has yet to be investigated in detail, and the absence of fifth and sixth century coins makes dating very difficult. For a summary of the present position see J. L. N. Myres, 'Britons and Saxons in the Post-Roman Centuries', *CBA Annual Report for 1961*, 35-45, and *Anglo-Saxon Pottery and the Settlement of England* (Oxford, 1969). Another important contribution to the study of this period is that of Dr John Morris, *The Age of Arthur*, London, 1973.

the answers must vary from one district to another.[1] When the rig and field pattern are identical, the former must obviously be contemporary with or post-date the latter, but there are many instances where an earlier rig can be seen preceding the field boundaries. It is possible that some of this type of cultivation may have originated in the Romano-British form of lazy-beds. These are ridges nearly 3 ft wide, dug out with the spade with furrows over a foot wide, and are similar to those now used for potatoes. But most of the ridge and furrow must belong to later periods and may often be the result of a need for improved drainage. Only large-scale surveys and a detailed understanding of past agricultural methods in each area will give the answers to the problems of this persistent and widespread feature of our landscape.

A common feature in some parts of the country is the marl-pit found on clay lands. The practice of marling the land, ie. digging out the clay and spreading it over the fields at regular intervals, was carried on into living memory and it was practised in pre-Roman times in Britain. Pliny refers to deep shafts in Britain, dug in the chalk which was then spread out on the land. Almost all the fields of Cheshire have their marl-pits which have become filled with water and are now useful as ponds for cattle. There are also many examples of hollows where ponds were deliberately made for catching water and dew, especially in Wessex.[2]

Habitation sites

Of ancient settlements and farmsteads themselves there is usually little trace except on upland areas. Notable exceptions are prehistoric hut circles in Iron Age hill-forts which have not suffered from the plough and many small enclosures of Roman and later date in the hills of Wales and Northumbria.[3] There are also the famous villages in Cornwall like Chysauster,

---

[1] The most important articles giving the various viewpoints are:

M. W. Beresford, 'Ridge and Furrow and Open Fields', *Economic Hist. Rev.,* 1, 2nd ser. (1948), 34ff; E. Kerridge, 'Ridge and Furrow and Agrarian History', *Economic Hist. Rev.,* 4, 2nd ser. (1951), 14-36; and 'A Reconsideration of some Former Husbandry Practices', *Agricultural Hist. Rev.,* 3 (1955), 26-40; S. R. Eyre, 'The Curving Plough-strip and its Historical Implications', *Agricultural Hist. Rev.,* 3 (1955), 80-94; W. R. Mead, 'Ridge and Furrow in Buckinghamshire', *Geogr. J.,* 120 (1954), 34-42; C. S. and C. S. Orwin, *The Open Fields.*

[2] O. G. S. Crawford, *Archaeology in the Field* (1953), 132-144.

[3] See the Royal Commission volumes, especially the more recent ones on Anglesey and Caernarvon. For Northumbrian sites see G. Jobey, 'Some Rectilinear Settlements of the Roman Period in Northumberland', *Archaeol. Aeliana,* 4th ser. 38 (1960), 1-38; 39 (1961), 87102; 41 (1963), 19-36; 42 (1964), 41-64; 44 (1966), 5-48; 46 (1968), 51-68.

hut circles on Dartmoor and the many interesting and puzzling structures in Scotland, the brochs and wheel-houses.[1] But in the lowland zones intensive cultivation has usually taken a heavy toll and we have to rely almost entirely on air reconnaissance. The task of the field-worker in sorting out some of these complexities requires much patience and skill is needed but aerial photography can play a useful role.

Prehistoric man in these islands was for the most part a wanderer, moving in search of new pastures and game, pausing only to sow and reap scanty crops. As soon as the initial richness of the top soil had been taken away new plots were prepared by clearance and burning. The increase of population and the resulting closer political integration during the Iron Age led to a greater degree of permanent settlement and with it the division of the most desirable lands into tribal ownership. There must have been in earlier times many skirmishes between groups of people invading each other's territory, but as soon as there are communities settled on the land and regarding it as their own by right of conquest or possession, the appearance of newcomers disputing this right takes on a new and deeper significance. The tribes were now prepared to defend themselves, their possessions and their lands. They needed the help of defensive barriers and the first widespread construction of forts in Britain comes in the early part of the Iron Age when people associated with the Hallstatt culture were coming into Britain after about 550 BC. The need for defences would have arisen not with the first wave of these new colonists but as the second and later waves reached these shores, probably a century later. The political and cultural complications of the period between c. 350 BC and the Roman Invasion are very great. The struggle for land intensified, and hill-forts, some of great size and complexity, proliferated as tribes and local overlords strove to defend themselves against their enemies who sought either plunder or conquest. These remarkable earthworks with their ramparts and ditches are to be seen on hill tops in many parts of Britain. Although they are so common, few serious attempts have been made to study and classify them, and their excavation usually requires such resources of money and manpower that it has daunted many would-be investigators[2] The last phase of many of the hill-forts was undoubtedly as a defence against the Roman Army but excavations have shown that in most cases

[1] For an attempt to solve some of the riddles see J. R. C. Hamilton, *Excavations at Clickhimin, Shetland* (H M S O, 1968).

[2] There is a useful summary of the present state of knowledge in *The Problems of the Iron Age in Southern Britain,* edited by S. S. Frere (Institute of Archaeology, London).

there are two or three or more preceding phases of construction.

The impact of Rome on Britain was very great. An entirely new form of civilisation was imposed which has left an indelible impression on our landscape. For the first time towns built on the Mediterranean pattern were introduced, with monumental public buildings fitted to a conception of town planning, water supply and drainage and commodious town houses for the wealthy tribal aristocrats and merchants. In the upland zones under permanent military control were the fortresses, forts, supply bases and signal stations, representing organisation on a highly detailed and vast scale. In the north the frontiers themselves took the form at different periods of two great barriers, Hadrian's Wall, seventy-two miles long and entirely in stone, and the shorter Antonine Wall constructed of turf on a foundation of cobbles. Connecting all these and other centres were the roads which have in all succeeding centuries been a source of constant interest.[1] Yet these great structural achievements have almost vanished. Many of the large towns and forts remained centres of population, and centuries of building and rebuilding have obliterated all trace of the hand of Rome. Very occasionally walls have miraculously survived as parts of later structures like the Jewry Wall at Leicester, the 'Old Work' at Wroxeter and the Mint Wall at Lincoln. At Canterbury some of the walls of medieval cellars are parts of Roman buildings and the constant re-use of defences until the seventeenth century has preserved much of the earlier work, though often only as a core and foundation.

Although there is much serious field-work and excavation to be done in our medieval cities there are still great possibilities of discovery in the countryside. All trace of some of the smaller Roman settlements has gone, although some are known by name, yet most of them had substantial defences. The great road system has remained the national pattern with London as its hub. Many of the Roman roads had been in continuous use throughout the Middle Ages though with only the barest maintenance. The turnpikes 'rediscovered' the earlier system, and until the very recent provision of adequate motor roads the Imperial Roman highways served this country well. Even so there are many Roman roads, especially the minor ones, awaiting discovery and most of those whose general routes are known need careful and detailed surveys. Of their history within the Roman period almost nothing is known, but where investigations have taken place

---

[1] Introductions to the period with extensive bibliographies are I. A. Richmond, *Roman Britain* (Pelican, 1963), and R. G. Collingwood, *The Archaeology of Roman Britain*, 2nd revised edition by I. A. Richmond (1969).

it has been shown to have been very complicated.[1]

In the upland areas sites have been better preserved than in the civil zones as there has been much less building and ploughing, but even here there are many forts still to be found and of the minor sites like signal stations almost nothing is known.

When one comes to the settlement sites of the Middle Ages, the problems become more acute. Only with the last three decades has it been appreciated that there is a need for medieval archaeology at all. While there are great standing buildings like castles and cathedrals with extensive archives which tell us when and by whom many were built and at what cost, some antiquaries see little point in wishing to know more. But the archives are not as comprehensive as one would wish and for a complete account one needs to probe deeper by field-work and excavation. There are hosts of sites for which there is only the vaguest documentary evidence. Everywhere, and particularly in frontier areas like the Welsh Marches and the Scottish border, there are small earth castles of motte and bailey type,[2] so many that the task of detailed survey and classification can only be done in modest areas at a time. There are many types and only a careful excavation of selected examples will help us towards an understanding of their origins and development. The moated sites of presumably later date are even more numerous and now have their own study group.

Scattered all over the country are the deserted medieval villages. A carefully planned attack has been made on their problems by field-work, excavation and documentary research, and although useful results are forthcoming, one feels that this is only a beginning.[3]

Many great ecclesiastical buildings were demolished under Henry VIII and many castles suffered the same fate at the time of the Civil War. They have received further depredations at the hands of nineteenth-century and early twentieth-century excavators anxious to recover the ground plans, especially of the great monasteries, without much appreciation of the problems of stratification and dating. We know relatively little of the medieval plans of most of our towns and cities. Apart from the few surviving buildings, all we can do is to look at the sketchy plans of the sixteenth

---

[1] The best general account is contained in I. D. Margary, *Roman Roads in Britain* (John Baker, 3rd edn 1973).

[2] For the difficulties in excavating such sites, see Philip Barker, 'Hen Domen, Montgomery: Excavations, 1960-7', *Chateau Gaillard*, iii (1970), 15-27.

[3] This valuable work has been carried out by the Deserted Medieval Village Research Group which publishes an annual Report. The Group has now listed several thousand sites. See also M. W. Beresford, *Lost Villages in England* (1955).

century and later.[1] Work on the ground combined with archive study could yield results here in the most unexpected ways.

Burial sites

Burial mounds, barrows or tumuli exist in great numbers all over Britain. Of all the structures surviving from our prehistoric past these have received the greatest attention.[2] Most of them have been plundered by eighteenth- and nineteenth-century antiquarians who dug into the middle to recover the primary burial with its burial urn and the fragmentary possessions of the dead. More precise excavation can today add more knowledge about the structure of the mound, the ritual accompanying the burial[3] and the secondary interments which the tumulus attracted in later centuries. There are even cases of hoards of Roman coins and jewellery being cached in them.

The mounds vary a great deal from the long barrows to the high conical tumuli of the Roman period and in detail hardly two are alike, but this is far from evident on a superficial examination. If they have not suffered seriously from the plough, earlier excavations and erosion, they are often covered with trees and vegetation. Stone structures such as cairns have often been robbed to provide building materials. Ground observation is therefore often severely limited and all one can say is that a mound exists which may or may not have been previously noted; it is surprising, in spite of the great interest in these mounds, how many there are of the latter category. The field-worker's task is to attempt to identify the true nature of the mound. It could be:

a. A grass-grown dump of material excavated from a nearby building or mineral working. Its irregular shape and nearby source of spoil should give it away.
b. A small glacial deposit.
c. A Roman signal station; but types with mounds are unusual—normally they were towers in small square enclosures.
d. Part of an early medieval ring-work or motte, which may include interior structures.

[1] R. A. Skelton, 'Tudor Town Plans in John Speed's Theatre', *Archaeol. J.*, 108 (1951), 109-120.

[2] Some of the best accounts are L. V. Grinsell, *The Ancient Burial Mounds of England* (1953); Glyn E. Daniel, *Prehistoric Chamber Tombs of England and Wales* (1950); Paul Ashbee, *The Bronze Age Round Barrow in Britain* (1960), and R. F. Jessup, 'Barrows and walled cemeteries in Roman Britain', *J. Brit. Archaeol. Ass.*, 22 (1958), 1-32.

[3] Sir Cyril Fox, *Life and Death in the Bronze Age* (1959).

e. A windmill base—these are quite common; post mills can be identified by the cruciform type of hole in the top which originally housed the foundation timbers. There would also be an approach road.

f. A gallows mound which would also have a hole in the top for the post, but there ought to be local maps or documentary evidence for this.

g. In stony country stones are collected from the fields and made into a heap; it may be simply the result of clearing the fields through the centuries of cultivation or a monument to commemorate some long-forgotten person or event, or an actual burial mound.

In the last five cases it is possible that a prehistoric tumulus was used if it happened to be conveniently situated, and only excavation can really tell.

There are many instances of the earth covering of a tomb being eroded or removed, exposing the large stones of the chamber, cist or gallery like the famous Kit's Coty in Kent.[1] Also one must include the stones standing as single sentinels or in circles as a kind of memorial, although some circles may have had other or additional functions like the most famous of them all, the Stonehenge sanctuary.

For every visible mound there must be at least four or five tumuli which have disappeared without a trace on the surface.[2] Some of these can be discovered by means of a crop-mark over the surrounding ditch. These at least can be plotted on maps and visited to see if any slight swelling in the ground indicates their presence. Around many of the standing monuments are woven local lore and legends which add to their interest, and these need to be collected and recorded before they are lost with the passing of the folk who remember them.

In addition to the single tumulus or group of tumuli there are the extensive cemeteries of various periods from late Bronze Age times. Surface indications in these cases are rare, and only occur when slight depressions may be shown up in a strong cross light. The field-worker needs scientific prospecting aids to map their extent once they are discovered (p 47).

Boundary earthworks

Under this heading can be grouped the various kinds of linear or

---

[1] In the eighteenth-century the outline of the original long barrow was still visible: R. F. Jessup, *The Archaeology of Kent* (1930), pl. III.

[2] The extent of destruction can be seen in the discovery of two large neolithic monuments at Durrington Walls and Marden in Wiltshire, each of which makes Stonehenge look very insignificant. G. J. Wainwright and I. H. Longworth, *Durrington Walls, Excavations 1966-68*, 1971, Soc. of Antiqs Research Report No. 29.

travelling earthworks. The simplest explanation of most of these features which consist only of a bank and ditch is that they were intended to mark out a territorial boundary. Some are self-evident like the medieval park pales usually enclosing a circular area and constructed to prevent the deer from straying. Some of them are very large and may well give the field-worker difficult problems in sorting them out. Many old woods are full of small banks dividing up various sections and only when they are followed, plotted on a map and equated to old maps and documents can a clear picture be obtained. There is endless work here for the field-worker as it is a subject which has been studied hardly at all.

The larger boundaries have received more study. Perhaps the most famous is Offa's Dyke, that remarkable boundary dividing English Mercia from the Celtic West. It has been the subject of a very fine survey by Sir Cyril Fox who has gone over it yard by yard with accurate and penetrating observation and considered its wider implications as a political barrier, not erected for defence but arrived at by treaty.[1] The student of these earthworks could not do better than use this piece of field-work as his model.

The following and plotting of these features is not difficult except where they have become heavily reduced, but careful observation is needed where they meet and cross other kinds of monuments, especially if the latter are of known dates. Field observation may tell one little and it may be necessary to take the spade and determine a relationship by a careful section. There has already been far too much useless armchair speculation about these boundaries; the answers are there, waiting for those who are prepared to take the time and trouble.

Industrial and mineral workings

Most of these are such a common feature of our landscape that hardly anyone bothers about them. Ever since Man started to build he has needed stone, sand, gravel and clay, all of which are found in this country in abundance. These workings are just as much part of our national heritage as the buildings themselves, yet it is very rarely that an archaeologist studies them as ancient features. It is more likely to be the geologist who is interested in the origins of building stone for a prehistoric or Roman site. Surface indications may give little indication of date. At Barnack, in Northamptonshire, are extensive medieval quarries known as the 'hills and hollows', yet the same stone was used in the Roman period. There can be

[1] *Offa's Dyke, A Field Survey of the Western Frontier Works of Mercia in the 7th and 8th Centuries,* 1955, originally published in *Archaeol. Cambrensis.*

no distinction between quarries of Roman and medieval date in the way erosion and vegetation growth has occurred, but there may be special features to be observed. The precise way the sandstone has been cut along the edge of the River Dee at Chester, Heronbridge and Holt has the hall-marks of a military organisation at work, and at Chester there is a rock-cut shrine to Minerva, preserved by its continued veneration as it was thought in the Middle Ages to portray the Virgin Mary. Along Hadrian's Wall the Roman quarries have inscriptions giving the names of the units and cen-turions who had worked them. Occasionally too the pits or quarries are conveniently near the construction for which they were intended, like the gravel pits beside a Roman road or an eighteenth-century turnpike.

Medieval and later documents may help in these problems but the only sure way is by studying the building materials themselves. It should be one of the tasks of the excavator to track down the source of all these materials; they are an essential part of the pattern of history and have a special bearing on economics and communications. The working of minerals for other purposes must also be included in any archaeological survey. The earliest are the flint mines and stone-axe factories.[1] Of the former the most famous are Grimes Graves in Norfolk and Cissbury and Harrow Hill in Sussex, but there must be others and one wonders if the strange tunnels in the chalk at Chislehurst in Kent are not an example, as well as some of the Dene Holes. Deep shafts and pits in the chalk may also result from marling or digging and spreading chalk or clay on the land to improve cultivation. Field-work has brought to light some of the prehistoric stone-axe factories but the starting point here was often an accurate geological identification of the rock from which the axes were made. This valuable work has been under way on a national scale and it has been possible to isolate certain areas of outcrop as potential factories.[2] Careful examination of the surface fragments and screes has resulted in the discovery of rough-cuts and chips at places like Craig Llwyd in North Wales, Great Langdale, Westmorland, and Mynydd Rhiw, Caernarvonshire.[3] There are other groups the rock of which has been identified, but the actual factory sites need to be discovered on the ground. Supplies of copper, lead, silver, gold, coal and iron could have been won from surface deposits and it is doubtful if there was much deep mining carried out even under Roman control. Open cuttings and

[1] Grahame Clark, *Prehistoric England,* 1940, chap. v.

[2] See reports in *Proc. Prehist. Soc.,* 17 (1951), 99; 25 (1959), 135; 28 (1962), 209; 30 (1964), 39.

[3] C. H. Houlder, 'The excavation of a Neolithic Stone Implement Factory on Mynydd Rhiw in Caernarvonshire', *Proc. Prehist. Soc.,* 27 (1961), 108-143.

mines are very difficult to date as it is rare that any traces of occupation or tools are found.[1] In North Wales there are occasional finds which indicate occupation by late Roman squatters at the entrance to artificial galleries and this may prove the mine to be of Roman or pre-Roman date. Stronger evidence comes in the form of remains of buildings on the surface like the baths and aqueduct at the Roman gold mine of Dolaucothi in Carmarthenshire.[2] In many cases all traces of the earlier workings have been removed when the ores were developed on a larger scale in later times. Thus there is little hope of ever knowing much about the copper workings at Amlwch on Parys Mountain, Anglesey. They were probably used in prehistoric times and almost certainly were under Roman control, but the whole of the interior of the mountain was gouged out to provide metal for the Napoleonic Wars and a fortune for its owners. The desolate site today has the appearance of a lunar landscape, tumbled, battered and scarred, but vivid in its colouring.

An area which might yield useful results through careful field-work and selected excavation is that of Charterhouse in the Mendips, the site of extensive Roman lead-silver works.[3] It might be difficult to sort out the earlier remains from the medieval but the opportunity is there and should be taken before it is too late.

Much more important are the Roman and medieval pottery works. They are of special significance since it is mainly by a careful study of pottery types that vessels can be dated with some precision. This is naturally of great concern to the excavators. At the production centres wasters can be found showing the range of types, and as the individual kilns could not be used for many firings their waster heaps cover a narrow span of time. The centres vary in size from the very extensive works along the Nene Valley, near Peterborough, stretched out over a length of ten miles, to one or two kilns constructed by itinerant potters for a local market.[4] Kilns are found by the surface scatter of pottery and fragments of kiln debris such as lumps of

---

[1] 'The Lead-mining Industry in North Wales in Roman Times', *Flints. Hist. Soc. Publ.*, 13 (1952-1953), 5-33, by the author.

[2] *RCHM, Carmarthenshire*, 113, 115 and 128; *Archaeol. Cambrensis*, 88 (1936), 51; *Bull. Board Celtic Stud.*, 14 (1950), 79 and 19 (1960), 71; *J. Roman Stud.*, 56 (1966) 122-127; *Antiquity*, 42 (1968), 299-302.

[3] For the Roman remains see *VCH Somerset*, i, 1906. See also *The Mendip Hills in Prehistoric and Roman Times*, 1970 (Bristol Archaeol. Research Group).

[4] Brian R. Hartley, *Notes on the Roman Pottery Industry in the Nene Valley*, 1960 (Peterborough Museum).

hard baked clay.[1] It is important that the field-worker should be able to identify these sites by their characteristics. Sometimes place- and field-names like Crock Hill or Devil's Kitchen are a great help, but they may refer merely to an occupation site. Tile kilns may not be quite so important but they also need investigating, especially the medieval ones which produced the splendid decorated floor tiles which help to date ecclesiastical sites. There are also lime kilns and corn-drying kilns which must exist by the hundred for the Roman and medieval periods. Once a kiln area is known, the sites of the individual kilns can soon be found with the aid of a magnetometer (see p 47).

The industrial achievements of the Middle Ages have in their way as important a part in the national scene as any abbey or castle but they are rarely documented and are more difficult to trace on the ground. A study of water mills and their effect on navigation would be revealing. The Norman mills on the Dee at Chester were directly responsible for the silting of the river which led to the decline of the port and the rise of Liverpool. The weir constructed across the river to channel the waters into the mill race prevented the flood tides from flowing beyond this point and so the natural scouring action of the ebb tide was lost. Many of our great rivers must have suffered in this and other ways when the Norman overlords established their corn-grinding monopolies.

But the greatest impact on our landscape came with the successive and mounting waves of the Industrial Revolution, which finally spewed the grim urban sprawl of the Midlands and the North. Only in recent years has interest been developed in the archaeological aspects of this widespread disfiguration of what was a pleasant landscape. Industrial archaeology offers enormous scope for the interested field-worker. There are special groups of keen enthusiasts working on the early development of the canals and railways, and roads have also received some attention, but docks and port installations do not seem to arouse the same zeal. The Research Committee of the CBA prepared a formidable list of possible lines of research including power mills of all kinds, iron works and forge mills, textile mills and those for associated works such as fulling and dyeing, mining in all its aspects with its underground galleries, surface plant and washing equipment, and other specialised types of industrial structure like pottery kilns, glass-houses and factories, early industrial housing schemes and the like.

---

[1] For details of structure see Philip Corder, 'The Structure of Romano-British Kilns', *Archaeol. J.,* 114 (1959), 10-27.

The growth of this study in the last few years has been remarkable; there are at least fifty local societies in Britain actively concerned with these studies.[1] Although much of the work involves the study of buildings and machinery, and thus demands from the field-worker a rather specialised knowledge of architectural and engineering drawing, there are vast areas of earthworks, slag and waste heaps, quarries and mined areas. It may seem a grim prospect to survey such remnants of the nineteenth century, but when combined with documentary and topographical studies it can become as deeply interesting a study as that of the more remote periods. There is an urgency for this kind of survey since many of the remains are being swept away in large-scale clearance schemes without a thought being given to their possible historical value.

Communications

This is a subject which can hardly be divorced from its period and has been touched on already. The Roman roads are an integral part of the pattern of the Roman military system and urban civilisation. A glance at the period map might convey the impression that there is little more to be known. In fact we may know the alignments of many of the main roads but even these have not been worked out in detail, and there are whole networks of minor roads and tracks to be discovered. Just how complicated the picture can really be is only appreciated when a detailed field survey is carried out over a small area. A few seasons' work could well greatly increase our knowledge and lead to the identification of new habitation and settlement sites as well. There is also the history of the system, about which we know almost nothing. It is clear that an enormous amount of field-work and excavation is needed before even tentative conclusions can be reached.

Methods of investigation

It should now be clear from this very brief survey of Man's impact on landscape that its detailed record, interpretation and historical assessment has hardly begun.[2] Bodies like the Ordnance Survey and Royal Commissions on Ancient and Historical Monuments have and are continuing to carry out work with increasing competence and experience but their maps and publications need to be supplemented by more detailed local or regional

[1] There is a quarterly journal, *Industrial Archaeology*, published by David & Charles, Newton Abbot, Devon (annual subscription £2.50), who also issue a large number of books on the subject, including regional studies. An extremely useful introduction is Kenneth Hudson's *Industrial Archaeology*, revised edn. 1966.

[2] An excellent summary is W. G. Hoskins, *The Making of the English Landscape*, 1955.

studies. There is thus ample scope for students with a general or specialised interest to use their knowledge and experience in the identification and classification of these earthworks and monuments.

Within this modest scope one cannot do more than indicate some possible ways of carrying out the classification and survey of field monuments. For the beginner this prospect is daunting enough. How can one possibly go out into the country and start identifying and dating earthworks? The answer is that one cannot do it without a great deal of careful preparation and it is almost impossible to start on one's own. The first step should be to join an active society whose members are already doing field-work. If there is no such body in existence in the area then seek the help of the local museum curator. These hard-working officials are often pleased to welcome the genuine enthusiast and if they cannot help personally, as they may be specialists in other fields, they can usually put students in touch with those who can. The first few years will inevitably be spent in training, with an active group or at summer schools if possible, and visiting sites which are well known and tracing out on the ground all the visible features. In this way one can become acquainted with the main types of earthwork on the ground and begin to recognise their characteristics. By then the student will have decided whether to attempt a regional study or concentrate on earthworks of a particular type or period. This will of course depend on the student's circumstances, in particular with regard to transport. If the student is an amateur working only at weekends there will be a limit to the distance he can travel. Specialised study can usually be carried out only by professionals either in the course of their normal work or in time devoted to research.

As this is intended as an outline sketch only, discussion will be concentrated on the methods used in a regional survey. The first task is to discover how much is already known about the area, along the lines suggested in the first chapter.

Perhaps the most important task is to become familiar with the Ordnance Survey maps so that by constant use they can be read at a glance as easily as the printed word. The scale most suited to field-work is the six inches to the mile. Although these maps are being revised fairly rapidly, there are still sheets which are 40 or 50 years out of date and more recent buildings and alterations to field boundaries will not have been introduced. Antiquities may be wrongly identified or not indicated at all. One of the first tasks of the serious field-worker is to bring his sheets up to date by incorporating all new information.

There is really only one way of doing field-work and that is by going over the ground on foot—it is quite useless to gaze at earthworks from the inside of a car or even from a road. One has to walk their length and breadth, look at them from all directions and ponder over all their features. This entails walking about on other peoples' land and it is essential to seek permission first. Most landowners and farmers if approached in the right way at the outset are pleased to help and often produce some unrecorded but relevant information, but to be caught unheralded creates difficulties which may prove ineradicable. It is essential that all archaeologists should respect the work on the land and its rights and properties; bad feeling started by an unfortunate action is remembered for years.

The work in the field includes walking around or along the features and observing their general shape and plan, and setting about recording them in detail. Often with simple earthworks one can take sufficient measurements by pacing and plotting them direct on to the Ordnance Sheet. One should know with fair precision the length of one's pace, and direct lines based on known points should always be used. For more detailed work a knowledge of surveying is necessary. This is a subject which seems to alarm students unnecessarily, although like all technical subjects it has its complexities once one starts on precision work with instruments such as the level and theodolite.[1] But most of the work can be carried out with ordinary 100-ft or 50 m measuring tapes, surveyor's chain and a few ranging poles which can be borrowed from a friendly surveyor or architect. The basic principle in surveying is to take measurements in a series of triangles, since if the lengths of all three sides of a triangle are known, it can be accurately reproduced. If one is merely adding information to an existing plan then one should choose two points on it as a base line and plot by measurements from them. When starting a completely new survey, the method is to build up a series of triangles one on the other to enclose or cover the features to be surveyed. If one proceeds in a systematic manner with carefully annotated drawings there should be little difficulty, although there are several practical problems to be overcome. In the first place all measurements must be horizontal, and on massive Iron Age hill-fort slopes this is not easy. Even with the help of ranging poles one needs to take each measurement by easy stages. Another is that of dealing with trees and dense undergrowth which cover many of our sites. When surveying ramparts and ditches the problem is to find where to take one's measurement.

---

[1] There is a useful little booklet, by D. H. Fryer, *Surveying for Archaeologists*, 1960, published by the University of Durham, but prehistorians may find R. J. C. Atkinson, *Field Archaeology* more applicable.

Where there may be a smooth continuous profile, points of maximum height or depth and intermediate changes of level have to be selected and followed.

For measuring profiles a simple type of level like an Abney clinometer can produce an approximate result. If a more detailed and accurate survey is needed one has to learn the basic techniques with a precise level, but with some instruction and practice the student will soon be able to carry out the work himself. The principles behind these methods can be gained from books, but for practical knowledge one should learn at first hand from a practitioner. The student should try to learn from the outset to make careful and accurate records, for if one starts with rough notes and thumb-nail sketches on backs of envelopes it is difficult to shake off these slipshod methods which will not earn the respect of one's colleagues.

Photographic records can also be very useful in supplementing a survey and giving a better idea of the present state of a monument than any description in words. There is so much photographic equipment of high quality these days that the main difficulty is that of choice. The best results are obtained from a camera which one can focus through the lens. Most of the reflex type take a 56 mm picture, but there are 35 mm cameras with a built-in retractable prism which permits direct focusing.[1] It is probably best to get advice from a photographer experienced in the type of records needed, then purchase a good quality camera and learn how to use it properly. When taking a photograph of a monument some kind of scale should be used and if there is no ranging pole available place someone at a convenient point. To see how skilfully this can be arranged the student should study the photographs published by Sir Mortimer Wheeler.

The survey of some types of earthwork need special techniques. Linear features traversing miles of country need to be followed with a disregard for other earthworks in their vicinity unless they happen to impinge; then of course their mutual relationships have to be established. There are notable studies in Sir Cyril Fox's survey of Offa's Dyke and I. D. Margary's *Roman Ways in the Weald* which the student would do well to go through in detail, observing the way in which 6-inch maps are used and the way profiles, photographs and field notes are incorporated in the published account.

The study and survey of Roman roads deserves a chapter to itself as there are so many pitfalls for the unwary. The beginner often assumes that

---

[1] For a good introduction to this subject see V. M. Conlon, *Camera Techniques in Archaeology,* 1973.

all straight lengths of modern road or lane must be Roman, and there is a grave danger of joining up bits and pieces of roads and hedges on a 1-inch map to make a Roman road. This is a form of armchair archaeology to be discouraged. One should start with a solid basis of fact such as two known Roman sites which would most probably have been joined by a road, or a substantial length of agger or embankment of known origin. The golden rule, as in most archaeological research, is to start from the known and work out towards the unknown. Remember also that Roman roads are not absolutely straight but usually go in straight stretches from one high point to another. Their alignments need to be tested by the spade, and as soon as this is done complications emerge concerning the historical development of the road system. This is the interesting stage and one is faced with the prospect of several years' hard and at times unrewarding work but, eventually, a few new pages can be written about the history of Roman Britain.

Work in towns has its own difficulties and problems. On the one hand changes have been far more frequent, but in compensation there are usually more records in the form of documents, plans, topographical drawings and photographs. There are still many medieval buildings hidden behind Georgian and Victorian façades and a surprising amount of structure survives in cellars. Professor S. S. Frere was able at Canterbury to work out the plan of much of the Roman theatre from lengths of walling he discovered in the cellars of fairly modern buildings. The thick Roman walls had been too massive to demolish so later builders had made use of them instead. However, one can sometimes be deceived by the re-use of Roman stones and it is not always possible to decide on the antiquity of walls by their appearance. When one is tracing the line of defences, evidence can be found in the buildings which have been erected over them. For example, attention must be paid to sudden changes of level and also to cracks in these buildings which could be caused by subsidence into a ditch while the rest of the structure rests on solid wall foundations. These and other tell-tale signs have special meaning for the trained and intelligent eye.

Aerial reconnaissance

Aerial reconnaissance has been the greatest instrument of progress in British Archaeology in this century. It began during the Great War of 1914-18 when observers in training in captive balloons over Salisbury Plain noticed that they had a much better view of the prehistoric antiquities than was possible on the ground. Suspended a few hundred feet above the earth's surface one naturally has a plan view, and earthworks whose

IIA   Air photograph of two conjoining enclosures near Stanton Harcourt.

IIB   A complex settlement pattern showing as crop-marks.

pattern is so confusing on the ground spring into shape, just as the plan one has so laboriously surveyed begins to make sense as it is plotted on the drawing board. But there is much more to it than that; very slight banks and ditches are accentuated by highlights and deep shadows when the sun is low on the horizon, so that features which may pass unnoticed on the ground are seen as a whole. One can, for example, see the main street of a deserted medieval village, each individual toft and the roads leading out to the fields. The slight sinkage in Anglo-Saxon cemeteries may show as a pattern of small rectangular hollows. The same results are seen after a light snowfall, frost or when there is standing water in the depressions (fig. 1).

Observers from the air soon began to notice that crops behaved in a strange manner at times and seemed to reflect in buried features their growth. It has been these crop-marks which have led to the discovery of many completely new and unsuspected sites in the last few decades. Although the results of aerial reconnaissance were well known after the 1914-18 war, very little serious survey work was carried out until the more recent war, during which great advances were made in this general technique.[1] In the last dozen years new discoveries have been flooding in at such a rate that archaeologists have not yet been able to take stock of the situation and only a small proportion have been excavated. The dates of whole ranges of sites have to be guessed on very general grounds and clearly the position will be found to be far more complicated once serious excavation starts, which may be a long time hence.

The effect of buried features on the growth of crops is basically quite simple but is more difficult when one tries to understand it in detail. The rate of growth of crops as well as the height of the plants will depend on the amount of nutrition the roots can gather and feed into the plant. Seeds cast on stony ground, as we are told in the New Testament, have poor survival value. Seeds cast where a Roman road lies a few inches below the surface are going to produce a very lean crop. So much is obvious. Where there are brick, stone or concrete foundations, walls and floors, two effects will be produced on the crop; its growth will be poorer and, in the case of cereals, it will ripen sooner than that in the rest of the field. These effects

---

[1] Among the works illustrating aerial photography can be cited Crawford and Keiller, *Wessex from the Air,* 1928; John Bradford, *Ancient Landscapes,* 1957; J. K. St. Joseph (ed.), *The Uses of Air Photography,* 1967; and J. K. St. Joseph and D. Knowles, *Monastic Sites from the Air,* 1952. Dr J. K. St. Joseph has published many of his photographs in *J. Roman Stud.,* 41 (1951), 52-65; 43 (1953), 81-97; 48 (1958), 86-101; 51 (1961), 117-135; 55 (1965); 74-89; and 59 (1969), 104-128; 63 (1973), 214-246. These are all Roman sites, and those of other periods appear regularly in *Antiquity.*

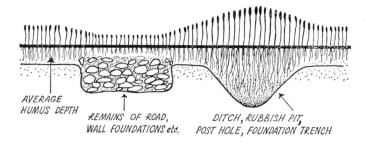

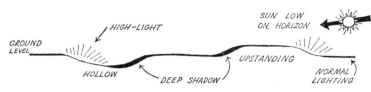

Fig. 1 The effect of shadows and crop differentials.

will be much accentuated if there has been a dry spell at a critical period of growth. The observer from the air will see the results of these differentials at the various stages. The first change takes place when the crop begins to turn from green to yellow. Where there are normal conditions in the field the crop will be green, but lack of nutrients will cause the plants growing over foundations to ripen more quickly and lighter lines and patches will appear and strengthen. At the optimum point photographs should be taken, for this effect may last only a few days and is constantly changing. Soon the whole field is yellow and no differences are visible. The next change takes place as the plants ripen and the colour changes from a rich yellow to a lighter tone; the differences will once more appear. When the crop has reached its maximum growth and another effect, caused by the different heights of the plants, may become visible. The stunting of growth may result in some plants being as much as a foot shorter than the norm. Shadow effects are now produced under low sunlight, building foundations being reversed into slight linear depressions and hollows.

Each crop behaves in a different way and its behaviour pattern has to be carefully studied by the air observer so that he can work out when the best effects will be visible and not waste flying time by constant patrol of the site. Barley creates an interesting effect, for in the final stages of ripening the ears droop and hang down at an acute angle to the stem. This difference of angle creates a difference in reflection from the sun but it

43

III   Roman streets and buildings at Wroxeter showing as crop-marks.

can be seen only from one position and may well be missed in a casual circuit if one is not aware of this phenomenon. The plants which have ripened
more quickly now show up as dark lines and patches.

Precisely the reverse of these effects is obtained if instead of foundations
there are buried ditches and pits. The moisture retained in them is much
greater than in the remainder of the field and this helps to nurture the
plants so that their growth is stronger and slower. Thus lines of ditches
show as green against the yellowing normal crop as it grows, or deeper
yellow against the lighter colour of the ripened crop, or as higher standing
plants. It should also be obvious that the greater the density of the plants
the sharper the marks created by these differentials. Sugar-beet for example
will give only vague and unsatisfactory results as the individual plants are
so large, whereas the cereals, especially barley, are extremely revealing.

44

Grass is one of the most effective but only under conditions of acute drought when the plants over foundations are parched out to a much lighter colour. Then one can occasionally obtain plans of buildings in most remarkable detail.

It cannot be emphasised enough that all these effects are very ephemeral and due to a special combination of circumstances which can be summarised as follows:

1. The type of crop, since each behaves differently under the same conditions of subsoil and weather.
2. The type of subsoil is the most critical factor. The better drained subsoils like sand and gravel will not retain moisture in a drought and this will help to produce the differentials of crop growth. It is very rare for crop-marks to occur on clay as there is usually sufficient moisture retained in the ground.
3. The weather is also critical. A fairly damp spring will result in sufficient moisture to bring the nutrients through the root into the plant to make the growth of even quality throughout the field. One needs a spell of dry weather just at the time when the young crop is at its maximum rate of growth to retard or hasten the plants growing over ancient features. But the crops in the next field may be different and the effects not visible at all, and one must wait until the special combination of circumstances create crop-marks here too. This may involve several years of patient waiting.

Crops under these conditions will reflect not only all the disturbance below ground but also modern agricultural methods. Aerial photographs show a bewildering number of interesting and mysterious marks and the beginner is duly cautioned against leaping to conclusions too quickly. The interpretation of photographs is an art requiring much experience and the ability to distinguish rapidly features which may be ancient from those of more recent origin. Most of the marks one sees in the fields are due to ploughing, seeding and reaping and will be aligned to the field. Tractor paths show up well, so do the patches of ground where manure heaps have stood for a short while the previous season. It is the other marks crossing fields regardless of modern hedges which repay attention. Consider a few examples of more recent activity. Land clearance may involve felling trees and grubbing out their roots, and the deep holes they leave will produce pit-like features; old hedge lines removed will provide a linear feature crossing the field; old quarries and sand or gravel pits which have been filled in will probably show. Then there are geological features still quite sharply defined such as channels in glacial deposits or outcrops of layers of differing rocks. The last war has left its traces in remote gun batteries and searchlight sites and radio and radar stations. These often produce circular and rectangular marks which can be very misleading.

After the war the Government produced for planning purposes a set of high-level verticals covering the whole country. Many of these flights were in January and are very useful for Roman roads and shadow sites but not for crop-marks. The detail is good but the height is far too great for normal archaeological use. These photographs do have an advantage in that they can be arranged as stereoscopic pairs. By placing two prints, taken at a rapid interval, together under a stereographic eye-piece one can see the contours of the ground magnified by the lenses in the eye-piece. This can be of considerable use in studying Iron Age hill-forts and similar large earth-works. Photographs taken by archaeological aerial reconnaissance are usually between 200 and 500 ft above the ground and are taken at an oblique angle. These cannot be used stereoscopically and they are also difficult to plot onto a horizontal plan.

The best camera to use for aerial photography is the R A F type F 24 which gives over 100 exposures and is steady. There is no need for colour (unless one is taking photographs to illustrate lectures). For publication one requires good quality monochrome in sharp focus. Cloud shadows should be watched as they can easily obscure the features to be recorded.

The real difficulty for amateurs wishing to carry out regular aerial reconnaissance is the high cost of flying. One need not be a pilot since it is very difficult to control the aircraft and take photographs at the same time; the observer-photographer should be concentrating entirely on camera work and directing the pilot into the right approach. The best kind of air-craft for this low-level work are the very slow types now regarded as obso-lescent, the Tiger Moth, the Auster and its variants. There are flying clubs up and down the country where keen pilots enjoy themselves in their leisure time. Taking their craft on short trips over their own locality tends to pall after a while and there is here a useful potential of intelligent people who might take readily to the idea of making fuller use of their time in the air. But one needs to start with the right basic ideas and avoid the expense of frustrating trips. The first requirement is a knowledge of the extent of the light sand and gravel areas from the geological drift maps. Concentrate on these at the critical periods of the year from late June to August. A great deal of patience is needed and it is almost akin to stalking timid wild animals in the bush.

Geo-physical prospecting

Just as aerial reconnaissance has revolutionised field-work in the survey of large areas, so geo-physical prospecting methods have radically changed the problems of site surveying. Until a few years ago the only kind of information an archaeologist could obtain about a site, apart from any report on previous investigation, was gained by what he could see with his own eyes. Some had their own methods of probing with steel bars or augers, others relied on bosing, a process of thumping the ground with a weight and detecting loosely filled features by the feel and sound. Professor R. J. C. Atkinson was one of the first pioneers in experimenting with geo-physical tools, yet when the first edition of his useful book *Field Archaeo-logy* appeared in 1946 there was no hint in it of these revolutionary techniques. Early work was handicapped by the dead weight of the large batteries which had to be carried out to provide the current for the electrical equipment. The invention of transistors during the war changed all this and it is now almost possible to carry a modest piece of equipment about in the pocket. These methods are not very new as geologists have been using resistivity methods to probe the earth's strata for the last fifty years; it is their application to archaeological problems that has been developed so recently.

There are two main methods to be considered, electrical resistivity and the detection of magnetic anomalies. The idea behind the former is basically simple. An electric current is passed through the earth between two electrodes and the amount of resistance measured on a meter. The resistance will depend on the features through which the current has to pass. Water is a good conductor, so the damper the conditions the smaller the resistance; conversely, the dryer the ground the greater the resistance. If there are buried features like pits and ditches they will show by low resistance but walls and floors will register higher readings. However, when one begins the operate along these lines practical difficulties arise. It is not satisfactory to put only two probes into the ground. One has to use at least four to avoid the difficulties of contact resistance when the resistance between the probes and the soil may be greater than that of the earth itself. The normal method uses four probes at equal spaces of two or three feet, either in a continuous series of traverses or on a grid system. Much of the early work by Professor Atkinson was carried out with a megger, the current being produced by a hand-generator. More recently instruments have been developed using null-balancing methods.[1]

[1] *The Scientist and Archaeology* (1963), 1-30.

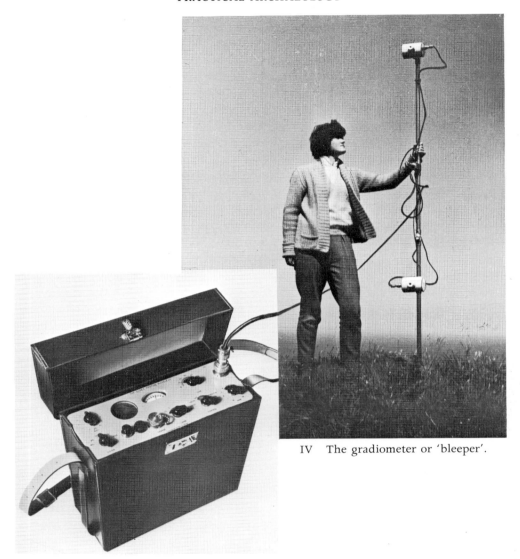

IV   The gradiometer or 'bleeper'.

The real problems begin with the interpretation of the results. The measurements reflect not merely the archaeological features which may be there but also the total earth mass, ie. the geological features below the subsoil. It is very rare that this will be uniform in character over the whole area. Most rock formations are very patchy: limestone may contain deep holes and crevasses filled with clay. Glacial deposits create even more difficulties as they change rapidly in consistency from clay to sand to gravel, with mixtures of all three. It is possible that small features of human origin may be completely blanketed out by these other more dominant characteristics. To attempt to allow for this one must have an ample knowledge of the geological conditions. The actual measurements in the form of a series of peaks and troughs do not always reflect the precise nature of the features. There are various methods of processing the data obtained from the readings to give smooth profiles to the curves, thus giving a truer reflection of the buried features. Detailed surveys should be the work of the geophysicist in close touch with the archaeologist, preferably while the work is actually in progress, so that the archaeological features discovered by the machine can be revealed and studied. The field-worker can obtain useful rough results on his own providing he understands the basic principles of earth resistivity. It is now possible to purchase a simple type of meter, adequate for most archaeological purposes, for about £60.[1]

The magnetometer operates on different principles, measuring the magnetic content of the subsoil below it.[2] The amount of magnetism over and above the earth's normal magnetic field will vary according to the presence of certain materials. Chief among these will, of course, be iron. The military use of mine detectors is well known; these tools are designed to reveal the presence of fairly large pieces of metal buried only a short distance below the soil. Archaeological features are usually deeper and much less magnetic. They fall into two main categories, burnt clay and the contents of pits and ditches. Most clay contains particles of iron compounds and when they are heated to the point beyond which clay becomes hard baked and loses its plastic quality, the iron becomes highly magnetic. Thus, even after centuries a buried hearth or kiln can be detected. Rubbish pits and ditches which become filled with humus have magnetic properties: the organic matter in the filling contains haematite, which is a weak form of an iron compound, and this is converted according to the degree of humidity into maghaemite which has the same chemical constituents but is more strongly magnetic. The enormous significance of this to the archaeologist must be immediately apparent. The discovery was made only in 1958 on the Water Newton excavations when the magnetometer was first used for locating pottery kilns, but since then this tool has revolutionised the work of the

[1] For example, the Martin-Clarke Resistivity Meter, produced by Messrs GeoElectronics, 98 Abingdon Road, Drayton, Bucks, in two versions, a very simple one for about £60 and a more sophisticated type for about £100 (1970 prices).

[2] The theory and practice is clearly explained in Dr. Aitken's *Physics and Archaeology* (1961).

excavator. The machine gives direct readings, can be used very rapidly, and in a matter of hours produces a comprehensive plan of all the pits and ditches on the site. As these features are the most important on many kinds of occupation sites the excavator can concentrate his efforts on the most productive areas.[1]

Geo-physical prospecting was at one time carried out by the normal type of magnetometer which is in effect a finely balanced magnet, but it has to be carefully set to the horizontal and in the earth's field. Another type of instrument has been developed by Dr Martin Aitken, of the University of Oxford Research Laboratory for Archaeology and the History of Art, the proton-magnetometer. This is a remarkably sensitive instrument which is also very simple to operate and covers the ground with great rapidity. The mechanics of the instrument are very difficult for the non-scientist to understand. It depends on the gyration of the proton in the hydrogen atom in a bottle of water. Normally protons precess or revolve about the earth's magnetic field. A coil of about 1,000 turns is put round the bottle and a current passed through this which re-aligns the axis of gyration of the protons. When the current is switched off the protons will in a few seconds return to their normal axis but the frequency will vary with the local strength of the magnetic field. It is possible to measure this as a large number of nuclei precessing in phase generate a force in the coil just as if a rotating magnet was present. The proton-magnetometer measures the frequency of a fixed number of proton gyrations through a crystal-controlled oscillator. The stronger the magnetic anomaly the more rapidly will the proton signal die away. The actual results are read as a five-digit number on dials on the magnetometer. This reading is plotted on a piece of squared paper representing to scale the actual grid over which the bottle is being moved from point to point at 2- or 3-ft intervals. It is then possible to note immediately areas of high magnetic anomaly. An acre site will involve at least 200 measurements and take about a day to cover once the main grid lines have been laid down.

The main difficulty for British archaeologists with this instrument is its cost, which is about £1,275, and which only large institutions like university science departments can afford. To overcome this a new and much simplified version has now been introduced. This is the gradiometer, known as the 'Bleeper' as it operates on an aural signal rather than giving an actual measurement (ph. iv). It consists of two bottles separated by a 6-ft

---

[1] For a geophysical survey and subsequent excavation, see the results from South Cadbury (*Antiq. J.,* 48 (1968), 8-10 and *Antiquity,* 42 (1968), 47-51.

rod, and the signal varies with the differences in magnetic intensity. If the rod is held vertically and there are no local anomalies, the degree of magnetism in each bottle will be the same and a steady note is heard. But when a magnetic disturbance is encountered the note is broken and the more rapid the individual notes the stronger the anomaly. The great advantage of this instrument, apart from the lower cost (£150-£200), is its simplicity in use—one merely walks about with the rod over the ground within the range of the cables. (These are 1970 prices.)

Another locating device, developed by C. Colani, is the Pulse Induction metal-detector.[1] It was devised originally as a sensitive metal-detector for both magnetic and non-magnetic objects. Strong, short current pulses are passed into a loop which produces strong magnetic pulses. Any metallic object within that field induces eddy-currents which can be registered. By using two loops of different sizes it is possible to make a rough assessment of the depth of the object. The sensitivity depends on several factors including the sub-soil conditions, but using a test plate of brass 100 mm square and 1 mm thick detecting was found to be possible up to 1·2 m and not less than ·8 m. Field experience has shown that the instrument, apart from certain limitations of depth, is as effective as the proton magnetometer in locating pits and other sub-soil disturbances, and more accurate since it avoids the southward shift characteristic of the magnetometers.

The disadvantages of the magnetometer lie in its sensitivity—the presence of wire in fences or corrugated sheeting in buildings is sufficient to affect seriously the readings within 100 ft. Overhead cables and electrified railway lines have an even greater and more disastrous effect. It will locate horseshoes, nails and buried scrap-iron, all of which may have to be excavated to be identified as non-archaeological features. There are also available some cheap commercially-produced pieces of equipment designed to attract the 'treasure-seeker', but they are of little value to the archaeologist.

Scientists usually deploy their resources and talents more rapidly than the archaeologist, who is often a lone individual with other kinds of problem in hand apart from his research. There is no doubt that new methods will continue to be found[2] and an additional battery of fine precision instru-

[1] *Archaeometry*, 9 (1966), 3-21; 11 (1969), 165-172. It is available from Messrs Geo-Electronics (see fn 1, p. 49) at a cost of about £100 (in 1970).

[2] There is a journal devoted entirely to prospecting methods for archaeologists, *Prospezioni Archaeologiche*, published by the Fondazione Lerici, Via Veneto 108, 1 00187 Roma (annual subscription 10 dollars). Articles on the subject also appear in *Archaeometry*, an annual journal published by the Research Laboratory for Archaeology and History of Art, 6 Keble Road, Oxford.

ments placed before the field-worker for test and development. As archaeology is still considered an Arts subject in most universities, the funds available for the purchase of these tools are very limited and the only way to solve this is a much closer collaboration with science colleagues, especially the geo-physicists who are now beginning to realise that some of these problems are awaiting their attention. The Department of the Environment, Ancient Monuments Division now has a section of trained people with highly sophisticated equipment to deal with sites threatened by development.

3. Investigation by excavation

Field-work and excavation go hand-in-hand; they are complementary and their relative value varies with the problems with which the investigator is concerned. By no means can every piece of field-work be conclusive however, and the ideas and tentative solutions to which it gives rise can only be tested by excavation. This is thus not merely a matter of finding things or of hopefully digging a site expecting something to turn up, but a carefully planned and conducted operation directed to attack problems to which answers are sought.[1] The problems are many and various, and may be divided for convenience into two main groups:

1. There are problems which concern the relationship of one type of site to others. One cannot, indeed, excavate without having this kind of relationship in mind, for hardly any site is unique. Barrows of the Bronze Age exist in their hundreds, and the main purpose of excavation of any given example is to see how its structure and datable deposits compare with others over a wide area, not limited merely to Britain. To take another example: Roman fort plans vary from period to period and for their understanding one needs to have in mind examples of their planning and internal arrangements from anywhere in the Roman Empire where they have been investigated. One could add indefinitely to this list. Every type of site of every age must be related to its fellows, the similarities and differences assessed and their significance considered. This broad view of archaeology can be obtained only by

[1] A philosophical approach is well exemplified by R. G. Collingwood in his *Autobiography*, chap. xi. For the practical aspects, Kathleen Kenyon's *Beginning in Archaeology* is an admirable handbook, and a brilliant general introduction is *Archaeology from the Earth* by Sir Mortimer Wheeler.

53

experience combined with extensive study of published material. Here the beginner needs much help in knowing where to find the main sources of information. It is this kind of problem too which constitutes the main justification for excavating at all, and at the same time it puts a heavy responsibility on the excavator to ensure that his comprehension of the site is sufficient to permit basic conclusions which will add to knowledge at this kind of level.

2. The second type of problem is that which is encountered the moment the spade is put into the ground, concerning not only the relationship between features and deposits as they are revealed but the chronology of the whole. In the past these matters were not always fully appreciated, but today no excavation can be considered as satisfactory unless the excavator can make a reasonable assessment, supported by evidence, of the period and circumstances of the laying down of each deposit and the construction of each feature, and of their general correlation. In other words, he must ascertain what was done where, when, and by whom.

Before considering methods of excavation in detail it is necessary to establish some main principles of technique and interpretation. Excavation involves the removal in a careful and systematic manner of all the structures and deposits created by the activities of Man and nature. The excavator must attempt to reach an understanding of all the events which have left their mark on the site and not merely those which engage his interest. The man-made features may range from walls and floors to hearths, from rubbish pits to post-holes and layers of different materials heaped up or thrown down for a variety of purposes—to raise a level,[1] to fill a hole, to remove walls for the re-use of stone or tile. In addition nature is always teasing the investigator with wandering channels caused by old tree roots and animal burrows. The task of the excavator is that of removing these structures and layers one at a time, keeping all the artifacts from each deposit in separate groups. The excavation should proceed in precisely the reverse order of deposition, ie. the last-laid deposit must be removed first, no matter how large or of what shape it is, and the process continued until the site has been thoroughly explored. Needless to say many of the more substantial structures, like walls, must be allowed to remain unless they conceal important evidence of earlier features. Most floors have to be taken up,

---

[1] Level can be a misleading word, since it should mean a horizontality but some archaeologists often use it to denote a layer or deposit.

but in the case of an interesting mosaic pavement this could be done so that it can be preserved for display in a museum.[1]

Another basic principle to be observed is the study throughout the excavation of the vertical sections which show the relationship between layers and features. If an area is stripped down without such sections, special techniques are necessary in order to record the vertical relationships as the excavation proceeds. It is very helpful to the excavator if a three-dimensional view is preserved of the excavation throughout. The full significance of the relationships and thus the chronology of the site cannot often be appreciated until the natural subsoil is reached. The various methods to ensure this are considered below.

At an early stage of his work the excavator must reach an understanding of the nature of the natural subsoil. In Britain the surface geology is remarkably varied, especially on glacial deposits. Much time and energy can be saved if the undisturbed levels can be readily identified. It is advisable at a selected point to continue one's trench or square well down into the natural subsoil to enable a thorough examination to be made. It is not sufficient to reach clean deposits—one needs to find bed-rock or its equivalent, the undisturbed natural subsoil.

Interpretation

If one layer effectively covers another, it can be assumed that the upper one is later in date, if only by a short time, or contemporary. In addition the lower one can be said to be 'sealed', ie. it is unlikely that artifacts could have passed in the course of time from the upper layer into the lower. It is possible for very small pieces of pottery and even tiny coins to fall through decayed root, worm tracks and cracks caused by sinkage. These can be detected by careful excavation and their significance assessed. There is a far more important principle, which is less easy to appreciate. Where a site has been continuously occupied and there are several major structural changes, considerable disturbance of the lower layers has frequently occurred. This comes about by the excavation for foundation-trenches and rubbish-pits and involves displacement of datable material. The later the layer, the more likely it is to contain residual earlier pottery and coins. On a Roman town site, for example, it is common to find a fourth-century deposit from which 75 per cent of the pottery is datable to the third, second and first centuries. As one goes back in time this dilution decreases, until

[1] It is now possible by using plastics to roll up a pavement like a carpet under suitable conditions but the beginner is advised to obtain some expert guidance through the local museum.

the primary layers of the very first occupation will contain only the pottery of that date. An exception to this rule is the layer where all the pottery is shown to be contemporary by the circumstances of the deposition, as when a building and all its contents are burnt down and left in position. All the pottery in such a layer will have been in use at the time of the disaster. The same applies when an army unit moves from an area and dumps all its stocks of pottery in a ditch or pit as part of the demolition and clearance. Pots accidentally dropped into a well indicate the time the well was in use, but these kinds of circumstances are rare. Almost all deposits contain rubbish survivals which should be discounted, and only the latest artifacts are to be considered in assessing the date of deposition.

Coins, because they can be closely dated, have sometimes been given greater significance than they in fact possess. If, for example, a coin is found datable to AD 41-54, all this really tells us is that the deposit could not have been laid down before this date.[1] One has then to consider the condition of the coin and assess the length of time it may have been in circulation before it was lost. This is very difficult and varies with different types of coin. There is the galley type *denarius* of Mark Antony, made of base silver, which was minted in 32-31 BC but remained in use in Britain until the middle of the second century, until in fact even baser silver coins were issued. This is an exceptional case, and all one can usually do is to estimate a life from 5 to 50 years by its appearance. But having allowed for this, the more important fact is that, in all probability, the layer was put down at a later date still, and unless there is more helpful evidence of another kind one must judge from the material from the layers above and below the one in question. The actual date of deposition after the making of

---

[1] Often the phrases *terminus post quem* and *terminus ante quem* are used (*post* means 'after' and *ante* 'before'). A coin which can be dated with precision gives an exact *terminus post quem* to the layer in which it is found; ie. it could not have been lost in that layer until *after* the date it was minted. The coin was struck, say in AD 122, therefore the layer could not possibly be given a date of deposition before this. But, of course, it could have got there at any subsequent date. This date, the actual date of deposition, is much more difficult to establish as the coin may be a rubbish survival in a deposit laid down centuries later than the mint date. The main agent for the *terminus ante quem* is the layer above the deposit in question. It is possible that this upper layer may give a date *before* which the lower must have been deposited. An example would be a deposit which can be shown to have artifacts in it datable to the time of deposition or with proved historical associations— such as a destruction layer of the Boudiccan insurrection of AD 60: a layer below this must have been deposited before this date. So these terms cannot be used for the actual layers themselves but the dating agents in and above them. They are confusing terms and unless the beginner is quite sure of their meaning, he would do well to avoid using them.

the artifact is often the most difficult assessment the excavator has to make, and many important reports published as recently as 10 to 20 years ago have now to be reinterpreted in the light of new knowledge. We all tend to make our choice in the light of our background knowledge and often find to our discomfort, as fresh information comes to hand, that our dates are too early.

Preparation

It is assumed here that the excavation is on a site which is either un-threatened by development or that if a threat exists there is adequate time for a full-scale investigation without undue pressure of time. If a director feels doubtful about his background knowledge and capabilities, he should seek out advice from those qualified to give it and should also try to ensure that such aid will be available during the course of the work. In this way problems can be discussed while the site is open and a wiser head may see features and evidence which has been overlooked. It is unfortunate that by a process of human nature, the young and inexperienced director tends to resent the advent of an older person who can tell him if he is making mis-takes and failing to appreciate the nature of the observable evidence. For the sake of the excavation, it is necessary for a touch of humility to prevail on both sides. The director should also recruit experienced assistants who can be trusted to deal with pottery, recording and surveying. If it is to be a large-scale operation the work can only be efficiently accomplished by team-work, and the less the director has to do of the routine chores the better for his peace of mind and concentration.

The attack on the site should be carefully planned as to sufficient re-sources in equipment and manpower as well as availability of the site. A few trial trenches merely tell us that a particular type of site exists, know-ledge which in many cases is already at hand. For the site to yield its com-plex history, a considerable area has to be stripped down to the natural subsoil. A Roman villa or country establishment of moderate size may need at least 600 man-weeks for a total examination. These may be spread accord-ing to circumstances and the type of material to be excavated, eg. clay will be much more arduous than sand. If one can devote only two weeks per year, this means twenty students each year for fifteen years; if a month per year, the time can be halved. The size, complexity and depths of each site will vary, but it is essential to have at the outset a careful assessment of the situation. Too often an excavator starts a site without a full appreciation of this and has to abandon his project before any worthwhile information is obtained. This is a waste of resources and may be damaging to the site.

The work prior to an excavation can be summarised as follows:

1. Finding out all one can about the site from published sources, casual finds in museums and local collections and aerial photographs as discussed in chapter 1.

2. Obtaining permission to excavate. If the site is scheduled as an Ancient Monument permission must be obtained from the Inspectorate of Ancient Monuments and Historic Buildings, Department of the Environment.[1] Landowners and tenants must be approached, and if a lengthy or large-scale operation is intended a good deal of tactful negotiation may be needed to avoid obtaining only a grudging permission which may terminate at any time. Most farmers are reasonable people and generally interested in the past, but the land is their livelihood and one must always appreciate this basic fact and not make suggestions which interfere with the cropping programme. One should offer compensation for damage and discipline one's team to use paths, shut gates and behave in a reasonable manner when on other people's property. These matters are elementary, but bad feelings have been aroused which can usually be traced to an unfortunate incident in the past when an excavator or members of his team behaved in a stupid or arrogant manner.

3. Another important matter which should be settled at this stage is the disposal of finds. All the objects found on an excavation are the property of the landowner unless they are found to be treasure trove.[2] Most landowners are willing to give the material to a local museum but there is always the possibility of finds which have a very high intrinsic value. It is only reasonable that the owners of the land should be informed of such finds and be allowed to determine their disposal. The archaeologist has to keep in mind the need to hold all material for close study and also to ensure that objects in a corroded state receive expert laboratory attention. This is why it is important that a museum is designated with adequate laboratory resources or access to them.

4. Collecting resources in manpower and equipment. If money is available, it may be possible to employ paid labour to do most of the heavy work.

[1] The *List of Ancient Monuments in England and Wales,* which is under continuous revision, is published from time to time by H M S O.

[2] This only applies to gold or silver and objects which have been buried with the original owners' intention to recover. The finding of all objects of these metals must be reported to the police to be brought to the attention of the coroner, who may decide to hold an inquest to determine the facts of the case. Treasure trove belongs to the Crown, except in some areas, and reasonable compensation is paid if it is retained by a body such as the British Museum.

Although it costs more, it is often better to use a contractor than to rely on casual labour from the Labour Exchange. There is now a growing number of people who make a living at excavating. Most of them are highly competent and work at a good steady pace in all conditions. They should be paid at the current government rates with the allowable subsidies for travel etc. This makes it awkward if there are volunteers on the site in addition and one should make this distinction clear. Amateurs are not welcomed by all directors since they may be inexperienced and unreliable and they may have to prove their competence and worth to the excavation. Sometimes a travel allowance may be allowable when the work is carried out by a local group or society on a purely voluntary basis. From these volunteers one needs to be assured of a permanent nucleus of stalwarts. Too often one starts with high hopes and enthusiasm, to find after a while a dramatic falling away. As soon as the novelty wears off and it is realised that it is going to be a slow and serious business, one is left with the steady, dedicated souls and there are very few of them.

Equipment needs will vary with the size and scope of the operation. Digging tools and surveying equipment, if they are not provided by the Department of the Environment, can quite often be borrowed from local authorities, and volunteers should be expected to bring their own smaller items such as trowels, hand shovels and brushes. The trowels should be pointing or gauging trowels, no longer than four inches and of good quality; blades merely riveted or welded to the handle soon come adrift. Among the items needed by the director can be listed the following:

a. Trays and tins for pottery and other artifacts—on most Roman and medieval sites at least two to each excavator.
b. Small boxes, bags and envelopes for small finds or items which need careful treatment and a fair number of stout bags for pottery after it has been marked and dried. If small plastic bags are used for metal objects, they should have holes punched in them to prevent the metal from 'sweating'.
c. Small labels, waterproof pens for marking tray labels, bags, and the pottery when it has been washed and dried.
d. Bowls and bristle nail brushes for washing pottery.
e. Note-books for records, and drawing paper and transparent plastic for plans, with a medium-sized drawing board and clips, pencils and rubbers.

f. Measuring equipment, such as folding rods, measuring tapes, a spirit level, a plumb-bob etc.

g. Photographic equipment. It is essential that a camera and film should be available at all times to make a permanent record of features or structural evidence before they are removed. The camera should be of a reflex type so that one can see exactly which features will be in the photograph and obtain a sharp focus. The use of two cameras may be advisable, one loaded with colour to record colour differentials, and also a good wide-angle lens (*f*. 3.5 24mm is about the best to avoid acute distortion) is needed and a set of extension tubes for taking small objects is a useful item. A set of scales of various sizes marked in metric lengths is necessary to give scale in the pictures and these can easily be made; ranging poles are normally used for cover of large areas.

h. Polythene bags for samples of materials needing laboratory study, and some polyvinyl acetate and brushes for cleaning and coating soft or crumbling material such as bones or plaster before removal from the ground.

Only when the excavation lasts for several weeks is it necessary to have all these items immediately available. On weekend forays, the pottery is usually bagged unwashed (here again polythene bags are useful especially on a wet site) the washing and marking being carried out later at home or in the museum. The requirements for portable finds on many prehistoric excavations are usually more modest; it is sometimes possible to contain all the material from a month's work in a single matchbox.

Trial trenching

If the site has no surface features, a preliminary stage after geophysical surveys could be a series of trial trenches laid out with the object of establishing the limits of the site and the nature and date of occupation. These trenches must not, however, be regarded as anything but superficial, as any removal of pieces of structure or deposits will be done in complete ignorance of their nature and relationships. Evidence may be removed in this way which could later be useful when judged in its context. The value of trial trenching will always be limited but it might enable a type of site of a particular period to be placed on a distribution map and this may add to knowledge. On the other hand, it may give an entirely false view. The site of the Saxon Royal Palaces at Cheddar produced a quantity of Roman pottery and a few trial trenches might have given evidence of a spread of occupation from an adjacent villa without a hint of the important Saxon buildings. There is no substitute for an area or open excavation and the serious limitations of trial trenches should be fully appreciated by all those who undertake them.

METHODS OF EXCAVATION

The types of site can be roughly classified under the following headings:

1. Small sites consisting of a single or a number of isolated features. In this category can be classed, for example, all tumuli or burial mounds and kilns for pottery, tile and lime. These can be completely excavated, but may require special techniques.

2. Defensive earthworks or linear boundary banks which can be studied by cutting a section at right angles to their alignment. The section gives only a vertical view of the sequence however. It is also necessary to strip an area, especially where linear features may be expected such as a palisade, the remains of which can only be studied in plan view.

3. Sites which contain buildings which might vary from substantial masonry to flimsy wind-breaks. These can only be adequately studied by complete horizontal stripping of the areas they occupy.

1. Small features

Fairly small features like many tumuli can be dealt with in a single operation, and the main objective should be to strip the most important areas and at the same time preserve vertical sections at right angles to one another across the whole structure. The normal practice is to use the quadrant method, by which segments are removed, leaving baulks, to give sections A-B and C-D as shown in the diagram (fig. 2). After drawing these sections it may be necessary to remove parts of the baulks to complete the excavation (ph. v). A barrow is a heap of turves, stones or subsoil but it may contain, at any level, any number of secondary burials. These will have been placed in the mound at some date subsequent to its construction. The primary burial may be associated with structures in the form of a stone cist or possibly with a timber mortuary house, or a deep shaft, and the perimeter of the barrow may have a circle of post-holes or stone kerbing. A great variety of structures and features can be found and hardly two are alike. In many barrows there are faint traces of an elaborate primitive ritual which are difficult to interpret,[1] and which are of vital importance to record completely. Barrows are also useful in enabling an examination to

---

[1] Apart from the books cited on p. 30, the student is recommended to the study of excavation reports in *Proc. Prehist. Soc., Antiq. J.* etc.

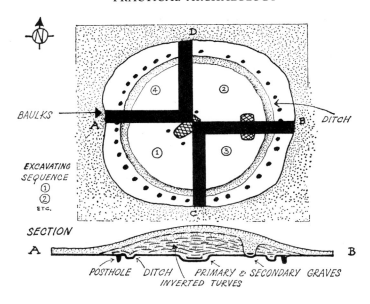

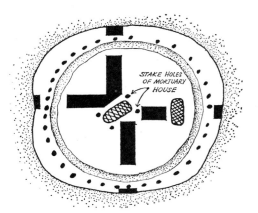

Fig. 2 The excavation of a tumulus by the quadrant method, showing two stages.

be made of a small area of ancient land surface undisturbed since the construction of the monument. Evidence of ploughing and hoeing may be found on the original humus if the ground has been cultivated.

Long barrows of the earlier Neolithic cultures require a special approach as they are large and elaborate structures whose internal arrangements and entrance can be very complicated. Some are in effect family tombs which were opened up to take new members as they died. Methods of excavation and recording require to be worked out in advance in some detail if all the available information is to be gained. Students should study the exposition by Professor W. F. Grimes[1] with his series of brilliant drawings to appreciate some of the problems involved in excavating one of these very difficult structures. It is certainly no task for a beginner.

On the other hand, pottery, tile and lime kilns are usually excavated completely at the outset. This is because it is very unlikely that there will be any stratification to study and attention must be concentrated on structural detail. This can only be studied as a whole and to leave a baulk across the kiln would only confuse, not help the excavator. These structures may be detected by magnetic prospecting (see p 49), as a box can be laid out in anticipation of the shape and direction of the kiln. But as this duly emerges the excavated area may have to be extended. The most difficult problem in this work is that of determining whether each piece of structure is collapsed debris or part of the kiln in situ. Sometimes each piece has to be carefully isolated to make quite sure it is not attached to a standing fragment. Pottery kilns are not only of great interest in themselves, there being hardly two alike, but the contemporary groups of pottery, in the form of wasters (ie. fragments broken in handling or in firing and which the potter has discarded), are extremely valuable in the information they give about the chronological development of local types. This information is most necessary when undertaking the excavation of neighbouring occupation sites.

2. Defensive earthworks

These are studied by means of trenches at right angles to the line of the defences and taken down through all layers to the natural subsoil. The two sections, one on each side of the trench, when carefully studied should reveal the relationships between the features. Ditch sections are usually more difficult than those through the rampart, and it may be better to tackle the work in two stages, dividing the trench at the front of the rampart or wall. It is not desirable to have unexcavated gaps in the trenches, however, as one needs to trace all the layers and features completely. Any attempt to divide the section and complete and back-fill one length before starting another therefore only results in creating unnecessary difficulties. One must never expect to solve all the problems in a single trench. Most defences can have a long and complicated series of structural sequences. A

[1] HMSO, *Excavations on Defence Sites 1939-45*, i (1960).

number of cuttings need to be planned at carefully selected points and the differences each reveals thoroughly studied. Unless the cutting is exceptionally wide, features spaced out intermittently along the rampart, such as a line of posts, could be easily missed. To avoid this mistake a selected length of the bank, of at least 30 m, should be totally excavated in addition to cuttings around the circuit.

The width of the trench

In setting out the trench the most important rule is that the deeper one has to go the wider should the trench be. The minimum should be 3 ft, (·91 m) and if the total depth is to be no more than 4 or 5 ft, (1·22 to 1·52 m) this may be sufficient. But for a 5 to 10 ft depth (1·52 to 3 m), a 4 ft (1·22 m) trench is the least in which one can operate comfortably. For more than 10 ft (3 m) one should start with a 5 ft (1·52 m) cutting. The best method of all, if the resources are available, is to start with a 10 ft (3 m) width for the first 5 ft (1·52 m) depth, then continue in a 7 ft (2·13 m) width for the next 5 ft (1·52 m) and a final 3 ft (·91 m) trench to the bottom. In this way two staging platforms will be created and the labourers can shovel all the material in relays. If one works the full width of the trench down all the way, shovelling out becomes too difficult after 6 to 7 ft (1·83-2·13 m) and the rest has to be brought out in buckets unless timber staging is constructed, which takes up at least 1 ft (·3 m) of the total width.

Timbering

This raises the question of timbering. If paid labour is used the excavator is obliged by law to provide timbering after 4 ft (1·22 m), and with amateurs it is usually desirable. The safety of a trench side is difficult to judge, and sometimes one can only know after an unpleasant accident. In normal trench excavation for sewers, cable and water mains the minimum width is taken out, and if the ground is at all loose close boarded timbering is supplied throughout, which completely masks the trench side. In an archaeological trench this would defeat the whole object of the operation, and careful planning is needed to decide on the minimum timbering and on exactly where it is to be placed. Usually it can be confined to the upper part of the trench, so that the lower levels where the most vital stratified layers are to be found will be comparatively free of obstruction. It is preferable for all the spoil to be dumped on one side only and this side with its added weight of spoil needs to be watched most carefully. Another danger comes from water seepage which tends to undermine the sides and cause their collapse. Timbering is really a professional job and financial allowance should be made to secure the safety of one's workers.

The excavation of a section through substantial defences may involve the removal of several ditch fillings and a rampart up to 20 ft (6 m) in height. Undertakings like these can be quite formidable and most of the work has to be done with pick and shovel or even a mechanical excavator. The method used by some German archaeologists has much to commend it. A trench is completely dug with a mechanical excavator, the sides trimmed and carefully studied. Another section a short distance away is then excavated by hand with complete fore-knowledge of what to expect. Each deposit can be removed in the correct order, and all finds securely associated with them. Unless a method of this kind is employed, it is very difficult to recognise and separate the different layers as one digs them out and, even more, to appreciate their archaeological significance. One has therefore to organise a system of recording which will enable rapid digging to proceed regardless of the stratification.

Recording finds in trench excavations

The method used is one of co-ordinating three measurements for every sherd found: 1. the distance along the trench; 2. the depth from ground level; 3. the distance from one side in relation to width. These three measurements indicate the exact position of each sherd in the trench space. The sherds are numbered serially as each piece is found, and this serial number and the three measurements are entered in a record book. This recording should be consistent, ie. always in the same order. The serial number is then written on a bag and the sherd put into it. A large number of small bags will be needed for this work, special care being taken when the sherds are washed to see that each is placed for drying on the bag from which it has been taken until it is dry and marked in Indian ink. There are one or two practical points which help to make this system of measurement more rapid and efficient. Along the side of the trench which is kept clear of spoil, a line of pegs is fixed about 18 inches (·5 m) from the trench edge and 5 ft (1·5 m) apart. These are measured in with great care, on a horizontal plane (not taken along the slope of the ground). The pegs (2 inches × 2 inches × 2 ft long) are so placed that either a particular side or corner can be used as the actual measured point throughout. In driving pegs securely into the ground the measurements can be changed by as much as an inch. To correct this small nails can be hammered in the top of each peg so that the precise reading is to the centre of each nail head. Each peg then has its position in feet painted on the side facing the trench.

All vertical measurements are made with a plumb-bob, and a ranging pole or stiff wooden bar is placed across the trench so that a vertical reading can be taken from any point in the width. It is usually found that a full-time recorder is needed for every 50 ft (15 m) of trench being excavated, unless it is a prehistoric site when finds of pottery are much rarer. The system can of course be varied if a large deposit is found in a particular layer, or if occupation layers are found below the rampart.

Once the section has been excavated time must be allowed for studying and drawing the sides. Any hurry at this stage is fatal to the whole enterprise, as the complete interpretation of main periods and relationship of all layers has to be established at this point. As one draws each layer or feature, so its relationship to other layers is established. This is the most important part of the whole operation, and methods of drawing and principles in interpretation must now be considered.

Drawing a section

The side of the trench or section has to be drawn in precise detail to a predetermined scale. The latter depends on the size and amount of detail. If there are thin layers of, for example, 10 mm thick to be drawn, the scale should be 1:10, but on a long section this may be impracticable. For example, a trench 250 ft (75 m) long would require a strip of paper 250 inches or nearly 21 ft (6·3 m) long! It is therefore advisable to halve the scale to 1:20 for exceptionally long sections. It is not advisable to reduce the scale any further, nor to attempt to break up the trench into separate lengths, as it is important to be able to establish overall relationships in defensive features. It is often helpful if the ground profile is first obtained, using a dumpy-level, levels being taken at each 5-ft (1·5 m) peg with intermediate points where necessary.

The most convenient kind of paper to use is graph paper on which there are five squares to the cm. If the ground profile has been levelled this is plotted first, then the recorder, with a colleague, starts at one end and works forwards until the whole length of the trench is drawn. The mechanics of this are simple. The recorder fixes a level datum line in the form of a length of builders' line tied to nails driven into the side of the trench. The best position is about halfway up, as long as this does not entail securing the nails into a stony deposit. One end of the line is fastened and the recorder stands in the middle with a spirit level on a drawing board which is held up to the line while his partner holds the line taut at the other end. The end is moved up and down until it is level and is then secured to the side. It is better not to attempt too long a length at a time (about 20 ft (6 m) is enough), otherwise the sag in the line is too great.

If nylon line is used, it is possible to work on a 50-ft (15 m) length. A measuring tape is now fixed, with the help of clothes pegs, to a nail or skewer at either end a few inches below the string to give the horizontal measurements. The position of the datum line is then plotted on the paper with a number of points at feet or metres marked for ease of reference. While one person plots, the other moves along the trench measuring off the positions of the various deposits above and below the datum line. After the actual lines of division between the layers have been plotted, the character of each layer is indicated by drawing in to scale the main stones, tiles and other large features and showing sand and gravel particles or whatever the constituents of the layers are. The use of colour often helps to bring out the differences.

The completed drawing should be as close a factual representation of the actual trench side as it is possible to obtain. It is also advisable to take a set of coloured photographs for record purposes, so that points of detail can later be checked against the drawing. To measure the various deposits it will be necessary to scrape areas of the trench side with a trowel to clarify obscure points. For this work a moulder's trowel is very suitable. For the beginner the drawing is a very difficult operation, as a totally inexperienced person may fail to observe all the lines which divide the various layers. If the trench side has dried out the differences become even less marked but can be brought to light again by judicious damping. The difference is often very subtle, and even when the experienced excavator points this out most beginners fail to see it. The art of this kind of work really lies in knowing what ought to be present. This does not mean a prejudiced view of the section, but merely an understanding of the various possibilities and a logical deduction of the train of events leading to the presence of the various layers. This cannot be taught in a book, but must be learnt by experience. Certain phenomena which recur in banks and ditches can however be discussed here so that the student can be aware of some of the problems they present.

Ditches

The actual shapes and sizes of ditches vary a great deal according to their time and circumstance. The characteristics of Roman military ditches, for example, are quite different from Roman civil ones and these in turn are not like medieval or prehistoric ones (fig. 3). This is hardly the place to start a discussion on the reasons for these variations, our present concern being with the changes which take place in ditches after they have been cut (fig. 4). Unless the ditch is rock-cut, the original sharp profiles are

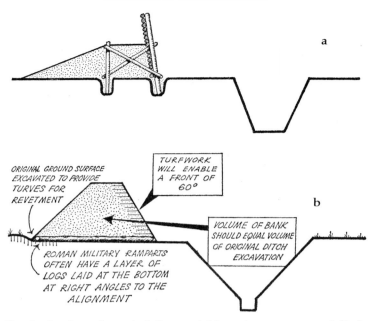

Fig. 3 Sections through defences: (*a*) Iron Age rampart and ditch;
(*b*) Roman military defences.

soon eroded or smoothed away, and the degree and rapidity of this erosion
varies with the character of the subsoil. The steeper the sides of the ditch
and the softer the subsoil, the greater will be the amount of material which
will wash into the bottom of the ditch. This is known as 'rapid silt', and
its depth will vary with the amount of erosion on the front of the bank and
the ditch-sides. The importance of this layer is that any pottery it contains
may be contemporary with the cutting, unless it has fallen in from the
bank or a much earlier deposit cut by the ditch. The rapid silt is usually
clean and sterile and closely resembles the natural subsoil. It is often difficult to detect the actual line of cutting into the undisturbed levels. For this
reason it is always advisable to excavate below the bottom and beyond the
sides of the ditches to establish beyond doubt the original line.

Erosion and silting are succeeded by a state of rest when vegetation
begins to establish itself. If the ditch remains open for a number of centuries, several inches of humus develop and these often show as a dark
layer over the rapid silt. It is of course much thinner on the sloping sides
and may be difficult to observe. On Roman military sites silting was
normally minimal as, if the fort was to be maintained at a high pitch of
fighting efficiency, the ditches had to be kept clean or periodically re-cut.

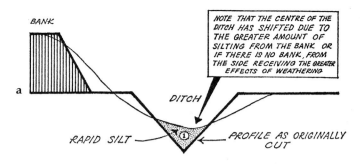

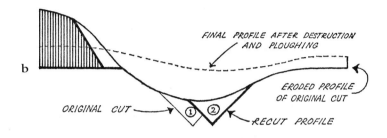

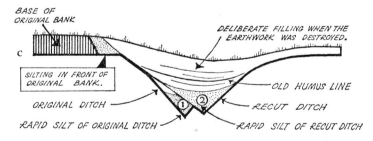

Fig. 4   The effects of re-cutting and erosion on a bank and ditch:
(a) as originally built and showing the effects of initial erosion;
(b) the effect of a re-cutting based on the eroded profile; (c) what
the excavator actually finds in this section.

The direction of the prevailing wind may cause erosion to be greater on
one side of the ditch, creating a shift in the centre of the ditch. If later
there is a re-cutting, it may be based on a new alignment, leaving the original bottom undisturbed (figs. 4 and 5).

At a subsequent stage, ditches may have been filled in by pushing the

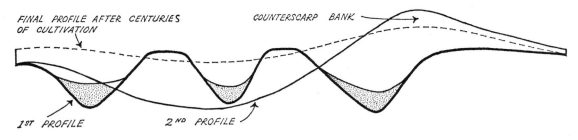

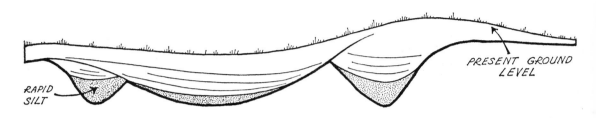

Fig. 5 A section across a ditch system: a Roman town wall ditch system, showing the effect of re-cutting a completely different system. The centre ditch of the first system is removed, and the spoil from the ditch of the second period forms a counter-scarp. The drawing below shows the section as seen by the excavator.

bank into them, but in time this filling consolidates and the ditches can be seen as slight depressions or swellings on the surface of the ground. This is often the case on Roman forts where there has been abandonment and re-occupation. An example of this occurs at Corbridge where the streets of the Flavian fort can be traced by the sagging into their side-ditches of later superimposed buildings.

Ramparts and Banks (figs. 6 and 7)

Ramparts or banks are barriers built up out of the spoil from the ditches. Occasionally material was scraped up inside the enclosure to provide extra bulk or height. The structure is therefore a dump of clean material, and one can often see in the section a series of tip lines where each load was shot and one can reconstruct the method by which the bank was raised. Usually the bank was placed directly on the contemporary ground surface, but there are examples, especially in the Roman period, where

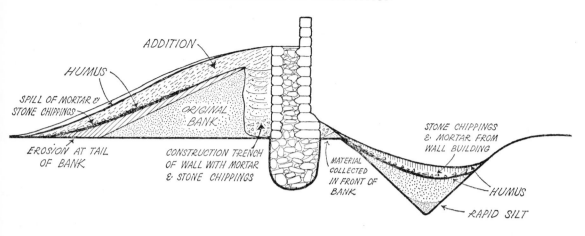

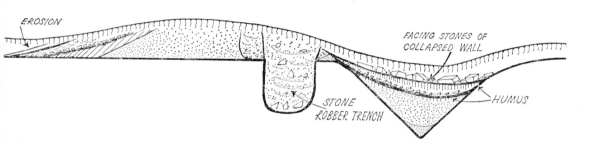

Fig. 6 A section across the defences of a Romano-British town: the effect of adding a wall to an existing bank, and increasing the height of the bank. The drawing below shows what the excavator may find, which provides him with enough evidence to reconstruct the sequence above.

this was first removed to give a better foundation and to provide turf for the revetment. In studying ramparts there are two main features to which critical attention must be directed: 1. the number of banks superimposed on one another; 2. the treatment at the front and back.

It is often very difficult to decide how many periods there are in a rampart, as the spoil is usually so mixed. The key to this problem is usually the presence of a dark humus line representing the turf growing on the

71

V   A section through the Roman town defences at Verulamium.

back of the first bank, before the enlargement; consideration of the number
of periods in the ditch system may also help, since each time ditches were
cut or re-cut there was new spoil to be placed somewhere. If there is only
one period of ditch construction it would be unlikely, but not impossible,
that there would be more than one bank. Conversely the new spoil may
not always have been placed on an existing bank. When Romano-British
town defences were reconstructed in the fourth century the material from
the ditches was usually made into a counterscarp in front of the ditch

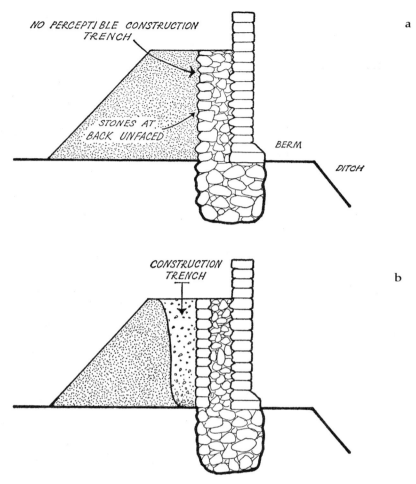

Fig. 7 The effect of adding a wall to an existing bank: (*a*) Roman town wall, built entirely from the front and inserted into an existing rampart; (*b*) Roman town wall, built into an existing rampart which has been cut back to enable the masons to face the back of the wall.

rather than taken into the enclosure to raise the height of the existing rampart. It is possible to work out the sizes of banks and counterscarps from the cubic content of the ditches since there should be an equation between them, and one can usually examine the full profiles of the ditches and at least the widths of banks and counterscarp. This is the sort of study

which enables one to carry out the reconstructions so vital to a full understanding of the true nature of the features under investigation.

The problems of the front are more difficult. The bank could tail down
to the ditch edge at the angle of slope natural to the material in what is
known as 'glacis' construction. For the attacker, however, a more formidable barrier was provided when the front was strengthened by other
materials to form a wall or revetment. This could be done in turf, timber or
masonry. Turf fronts were often used by the Roman Army; the turves,
cut to a standard size, were stacked grass to grass at the front and back of
the rampart and the softer ditch filling dumped in the middle. The front
was rarely vertical, but could be built to an angle of about 60°. It was not
very durable but started to disintegrate after several decades[1] and was
difficult to reface in turf; it was more often replaced by masonry. Turfwork
can usually be recognised in a section by the alternating black or dark
grey bands, the individual turves having been compressed in the course
of time from the original 6 to 12 inches to 2 to 3 inches.

Timber revetments took a great variety of forms and some of the ramparts of Iron Age hill forts are of extremely complicated construction.[2]
The Roman military method was often to cut a palisade trench along the
front of the bank, into which massive uprights were inserted to support the
bank and the bratticing on the patrol track along the top of the rampart.
The same effect was also achieved with posts at regular intervals of five or
more feet without the connecting trench. There is a danger here that the
excavator may site his trench between posts, and, if timber work of this
kind is suspected, it may be as well to open the rampart front to a length of
at least 10 ft. All the timbers themselves will have decayed and left only
ghostly shadows of their presence except in waterlogged conditions when
the stumps may have been preserved. Sometimes the fronts were dismantled and only the post-holes or palisade trench left below ground.
Walls are certainly the easiest features to recognise, although they have
often been completely robbed out for their stone and tiles. The relationship
between bank and wall may be a problem as it cannot always be assumed
that the two are contemporary. There are three possibilities: 1. The wall
was built first before the bank was heaped up and therefore the ditches
dug. In such a case the wall will have faced masonry on both sides and

[1] A turf rampart has been built by Mr B. Hobley at the Roman fort at Baginton, near
Coventry, and this experience has shown that the front does not deteriorate greatly once it
has become grassed over.

M. Aylwin Cotton, 'British Camps with Timber-laced Ramparts', Archaeol. J., 3
(1955), 26-105.

there will be a strew of masons' chippings and mortar below the rampart. 2. The wall and bank were built together as part of one general operation but it would have been unusual if the masons and ditch diggers had worked at exactly the same speed for the whole of the circuit. Evidence for this is again the layers of mortar and stone which may be found at several stages in the tip lines of the bank. An interior face to the wall would be unnecessary in this instance, and its absence would be an indication. 3. The wall was inserted into the front of the bank, in which case the front would have been cut back to provide the masons with room to work and this construction trench, as it is called, would have been back-filled later on. But this would only be necessary if the back face of the wall was to be of faced masonry or if timber formwork was needed, as in the case of the Roman flint and mass-concrete walls of Colchester, Silchester and Verulamium. It is possible to build a substantial wall entirely from the front by laying courses of stones against the cut-back face of the bank, but it would then be impossible to strike the joints with a pointing trowel and the mortar would be squeezed out and project from the face of the wall. In this type of construction there need be no construction trench at all, only a very small gap between the wall and the bank.

Although it may be a simple matter to decide that this was the sequence of events, it is much more difficult to determine whether it was all done as part of a general scheme or whether the wall was an insertion at a later date. The only answer to this riddle may lie in the pottery from the construction trench, if one was cut, but this may include material cut away from the front of the bank and is unlikely to contain any sherds from other sources. It is also unlikely that enough will have survived of the top of the bank to make possible an examination of the relationship between the turf line on the bank and the construction trench. A critical point may be the front of the wall where the outer edge of the construction trench may have cut into layers which had collected in front of the bank while it was in a state of slow erosion.

These illustrations should help to show the kinds of possibility which may exist but there are hardly two examples alike and much careful observation and thought is necessary before a solution can be advanced. Although the examples have been chosen from the Roman period, the main principles apply to prehistoric and medieval defences. The excavator should be familiar with the possibilities each period may present.

3. Excavating an area

The problems involved in excavating areas of occupation are far more varied and complex than any other type of excavation. It is impossible to give instructions on every eventuality, but there are basic techniques which can be applied to most types of site. At the start of an excavation when there are people present only too anxious to put spades into the ground, there may be a tendency to set out areas quickly without due thought and care. Serious mistakes can be made at this stage. The directing staff should be present on the site at least a day ahead of everyone else, and talk over all the problems. In open excavation all the spoil has to be taken away in barrows or dumpers. The choice of the site for the dump is critical. It must be in a place where there is no need to excavate immediately or in that season, and it must also be as near as possible for economy of labour. Another factor is the possibility of the spoil or part of it (especially if it is good quality humus) being removed from the site altogether if the excavation is prior to any development. If this is not part of the stripping operation the dump should be accessible to vehicles and room must be left for loading. One should also plan the sites for the essential huts for directing staff, for storage and as places for the workers to eat. If some of the workers are camping on the site space should be available for them also with cooking areas and latrines carefully placed. The operation centre should be near to and overlooking the excavation, but also if possible by the main access to the site from nearby public streets or roads.

Grass is by far the best surface from which to excavate, but it needs scything or cutting before a start is made. It gives a clean hard edge to the sides of the area and can be brushed clean and kept tidy. Tidiness is as much in place in an excavation as in a scientific laboratory, but need not become a fetish. The old-fashioned method of setting the site out on a grid and excavating in squares does not allow a proper excavation of the structures in their entirety. One needs to examine the contemporary occupation of a whole building or significant part of a building. It is impossible to do this if there are baulks and the building is deep. On a 3 m (10 ft) square grid the baulks can occupy at least a third of the area investigated, but they have their uses. They preserve the vertical stratification and provide ways across the site without walking over the excavated areas. It may be desirable at the beginning to leave some baulks; which can be removed later when they interfere with the study of the structures.

Open stripping (ph. vi)

The only satisfactory method of excavating is by stripping large areas at a time. Each layer and feature can be examined individually and cleared completely. The value of this system was first shown on two large-scale

VI   An example of excavation by open stripping at Winchester.

emergency excavations which demonstrated the presence in Britain of timber buildings of a type not previously known, and it is certain that if these sites had merely been examined, as in the past, by a few trial trenches, these buildings would never have been found. Archaeologists in Britain had for some time been puzzled by the apparent absence of any substantial timber structures of the Saxon period, whereas on the Continent the plans of complete villages have been recovered with several different types of buildings.[1] The work of Dr Brian Hope-Taylor at Yeavering, Northumberland, and Mr Philip Rahtz at Cheddar, Somerset, admittedly on royal palaces,[2] have shown us the answer to this problem. It was necessary to strip large areas completely and to study and classify the types of postholes before being able to complete the plan of this kind of building. In Britain until recently there had very rarely been the resources for large-scale excavation of this kind, until the Government intervened on the threatened sites mentioned above and by great fortune appointed as directors excavators of great technical skill. Trenching or even gridding such sites, however carefully done, would never have shown enough of their plan to permit adequate interpretation. The technique has been developed on a number of excavations, the most important of which have undoubtedly been those in the City of Winchester under the direction of Mr Martin Biddle[3] (ph. v), and on a more modest scale, by Mr Philip Barker on a timber castle site at Hen Domen, Montgomery. Other examples are by Mr Philip Rahtz at King John's Hunting Lodge at Writtle, Essex[4] and Mr Barker on part of the bath-house in the Roman town at Wroxeter.[5] The technique has now become widely practised.

This technique is particularly suited to medieval houses, the rough stone foundations of which were simply placed on the ground. Occasionally enough of the stone-work survives to provide the excavator with a sound plan.[6] Often, however, the stones have been too much disturbed by robbing

---

[1] C. A. Ralegh Radford, 'The Saxon House: a review and some parallels', *Medieval Archaeol.*, 1 for 1957 (1958), 27-38.

[2] The reports on these two important excavations have not yet been published.

[3] The results have appeared in brief interim reports in *Antiq. J.*, 44 (1964), 188-219; 45 (1965), 230-264; 46 (1966), 308-332; 47 (1967), 251-279; 48 (1968), 250, 284; and a discussion of the method is given in *World Archaeol.*, 1 (1969), 208-219).

[4] *Soc. Medieval Archaeol.*, Monograph: No. 3, 1969.

[5] *World Archaeol.*, 1 (1969), 220-235; *Excavations on the site of the Bath Basilica at Wroxeter 1966-71* and *1972*.

[6] As at Beere, see 'Excavation of a Medieval Settlement at Beere, North Tawton, Devon', by E. M. Jope and R. I. Threlfall, *Medieval Archaeol.*, 2 for 1958 (1959), 112-140, and 'A Monastic Homestead on Dean Moor, S. Devon' by Aileen Fox, *ibid.*, 141-157.

VII Excavating by open stripping on the site of a Saxon palace at Cheddar.

and the plough, and only by very careful plotting of all stones at different levels is it possible to arrive at any conclusion at all. This method, first developed by Axel Steensberg in Denmark,[1] has been successfully applied in this country by Mr John Hurst and Mr Philip Rahtz on deserted medieval villages.[2] In the case of timber buildings open stripping is the only method which will reveal their plan. Where timbers have been put into the ground either vertically or horizontally the places they occupied can often be traced by the holes and trenches originally dug for them. Where, however, they have been merely laid over the original ground surface there will be no evidence except a difference in the surfaces inside and outside the building, the lines of small stones which collected against the walls when they were standing and the effect of water running off the roof.

The classic excavation of the technique on a late prehistoric farmstead was that by Professor G. Bersu at Little Woodbury, Wilts.[3] The greater part of this site was stripped and each feature isolated and sectioned with extreme precision, enabling imaginative attempts at reconstruction to be made.

Excavation techniques

Having determined the area to be stripped and the sites of spoil dumps, huts, stores etc, the next task is to set out a recording grid round the edges. If the site is a level one and fairly free of stone the detailed survey can be greatly aided by setting out a grid all over the site with thin steel rods. These are driven into the ground until they are quite firm at intervals of 2 m. Labels are attached to each rod giving its grid co-ordinate. Thus in the diagram the rod at A would be 0404 and at B 1210 (fig. 8) Once accurately established, such a grid enables surveying to proceed rapidly. With the help of metre measuring rods one can also record all significant finds by extending the system of co-ordinates; thus a find at C could simply be recorded as 128053 with the addition of the layer number. Some excavators prefer to leave the setting out of the grid until they know the main axes of the buildings being excavated, but this may mean serious delay.

The next task is to strip off the top soil, which may be grass and humus or plough soil and may vary considerably in depth from 6 inches (*c.* 15 cm)

[1] A. Steensberg, *Farms and Water-mills in Denmark during 2,000 Years*, Copenhagen 1952.

[2] J. G. Hurst, 'Deserted Medieval Villages and the Excavations at Wharram Percy, Yorks' *Recent Archaeological Excavations in Britain*, 1956; R. H. Hilton and P. A. Rahtz, 'Upton, Glos, 1959-64', *Trans. Bristol. and Glos. Archaeol. Soc.*, 85 (1966), 70-146; 88 (1969), 74-126; see also M. W. Beresford, *The Lost Villages of England* (1954).

[3] *Proc. Prehist. Soc.*, 6 (1940), 30.

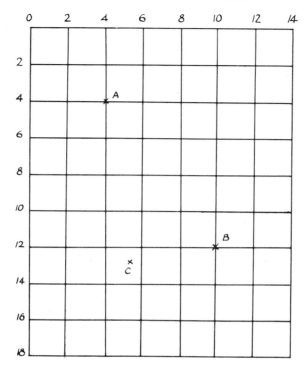

Fig. 8   Recording grid.

to 3 ft (*c*. 1 m). The surface now reached should be carefully cleaned and studied. This is the latest available archaeological horizon. It has probably been disturbed by vegetation and ploughing but there is a chance that it is a view of the site in its last stage of abandonment. It should be possible to decide whether any buildings merely collapsed as they decayed through neglect, or were destroyed by accidental conflagration, or were demolished and the building materials removed. Only the examination of an area of at least 50 sq ft (*c*. 70 sq m) could produce enough evidence to support any such conclusions. If there are features to be recorded it is now necessary to draw a plan and take photographs. With the grid already in position, a survey can be done rapidly with the help of lines strung across the site from the pegs, extending the grid physically over the area or by using a portable grid aligned to the system (ph. vi). Not only does each feature need to be drawn but so does every stone and change of surface texture. The survey should, if possible, be supplemented by vertical photographs taken with the aid of a portable tripod and aligned to the grid.

81

Having examined the uppermost surviving layer, a decision has to be taken on how next to proceed. It will be necessary to have vertical sections along selected lines, even possibly in the form of baulks. But the problem is that of siting these lines before the main buildings have been located, since it is unlikely that they will appear after the stripping of the humus or plough-soil. When in doubt it is advisable to lay down rather more section lines than may be ultimately necessary. If the excavation is to be total, ie. no baulks left in at all, then the sections can only be built up layer by layer and they never will be actually seen in position. This will become clearer when the method is described in detail. A horizontal line is carefully set out over the area along the agreed section line and excavation proceeds on one side of this line only, leaving the highest layer intact along the section line. To take the simplest case, if only one section is to be drawn, then a line may be set out halfway across the area. In this case in only one half is the next layer excavated and then the section revealed is drawn in relation to the horizontal line above it; after this the other half of the layer is stripped until the whole area is reduced by one layer. When the layers are very thin this technique is extremely difficult and it may be necessary to take several layers away before there is any vertical section to be drawn.

This technique requires not only skill but flexibility of method and above all experience. Mistakes at the beginning of an excavation are inevitable and one has to adapt the methods to fit the problems of the site. The old-fashioned grid could be applied rigidly and sites dug in a regimented way without any real understanding of the archaeology of the site. One of the advantages of the open method is that it forces the director or supervisor to think out constantly what he is doing. The real difficulty is that of deciding precisely where each layer begins and ends, since it will become apparent that there are patches or areas of differing materials and also features which will usually stand out as areas of different colour or texture; these may represent hearths, ovens, post-holes, gulleys or pits. All these have to be carefully emptied individually. An excellent example of this kind of technique is at Hen Domen, where Mr Phil Barker's plan of the phase Y, the penultimate surface, shows features which can be interpreted as buildings (fig. 22), but which are very difficult to determine.

Recording layers

The making of adequate records as the excavation proceeds is something that tends to worry the conscientious amateur who is trying to do the work properly. Some make so much of it that it becomes an end in itself and the more important aspects of the work are overlooked. The solution is to have a simple routine which proceeds automatically. Also it is usually advisable to have an experienced person whose main responsibility it is to see that the job of recording all finds is being carried out properly.

Records can take various forms, from photographs to measured drawings and notes. The methods adopted will differ according to circumstances. In small-scale excavations it can all be done by the directing staff, but on a complicated building site where there is a large area being developed at the same time, it is advisable to give each area a separate sequence of record books.

In excavating a grid the recording of finds is made easy by giving each square a separate record book. The same method can be applied to the open method provided the area is covered with a recording grid. A separate book can be provided for each 2 m or 4 m square but there must be close co-ordination over the whole area to ensure ease of identification of all the layers. If the given example is used (p. 81) there are sixty-three 2 m squares; one could have had in the former system sixty-three different numbers for a layer which covered the whole side. A system of conflation must be adopted and entered into each book at the end. On the other hand many small layers or features will be peculiar to each square and numbered independently. One of the excavators, preferably a person with legible handwriting, is given the responsibility of the record book, but a master record is also needed for the whole area to make sure that the entries are comprehensive and also to provide the essential links between each area.

The record book should be used for two kinds of information, the numbering and description of the layers and features, and accurate scale drawings of all features such as hearths and pits which have to be removed during the excavation. It may be useful to paste in appropriate photographs. The kind of book most suitable for this is one in which pages of lined and squared paper are interleaved. All record books should be of the same type and of good quality with stiff covers; cheap exercise books deteriorate and do not encourage good records.

There are several methods of numbering and recording layers and features. The director must have a simple method carefully worked out in advance and keep to it throughout the excavation. It must therefore be a system capable of limitless expansion, and it should also be borne in mind that the figures and numbers used will be written on every sherd of pottery and therefore need to be fairly short. It is useful too if the formula is meaningful and denotes a precise layer at a precise point in the excavation. The following system is offered as a straightforward example which has stood the test of many excavations. It consists of three factors:

1. Two letters denoting the name of the site, eg. WB stands for Wroxeter Baths; another site at Wroxeter would be given a different key letter.
2. A serial number in a circle to denote the number of the square, trench or area on the site.
3. Another serial number to denote the number of the layer in that particular square, trench or area.

Thus a full example of a layer number might be WB ⑥ 51, which means the fifty-first layer, in square or area 6, at Wroxeter Baths. Some like to add the year which may be important if the excavation is to proceed for a number of years, but it is easier to make this entry in the record book.

It is desirable to have a different system of enumeration for features. These include all man-made structures such as hearths, post-holes, wells, pits, construction trenches and walls etc. They form a series which is also entered in the record book. The simplest way of doing this is by adding the letter F to the number. This is for the convenience of drawing plans and sections and taking photographs. Thus, for every area for which there is a separate record book, there will also be a separate numerical sequence of features: if one wishes to refer to a particular feature out of the context of its area the site letters and area number can be added. This system does not replace the layer number. As each feature is excavated it may produce its own sequence of layers which are numbered in the layer number series. It is a great convenience to be able when deciding layers to be able to refer to a feature number. Some excavators give different sequences to each kind of feature and have for example a series for pits and another for post-holes etc. This refinement may lead to difficulties when identification is not immediate. It is not always possible to know that a post-hole is not a pit and *vice versa*. But it may be convenient to give a special sequence to walls and a practice has arisen of distinguishing these by means of Roman numerals.

At the end of a season a line is ruled across and at the beginning of the next, the date entered. At the same time a note should be written on the state of the work on any area or square which is unfinished. This is necessary as the excavation is normally back-filled to protect the exposed areas and features from frost.

It is important that the treatment of the record book should be systematised and this could take the form of an instruction pasted on the cover of all record books. An example might serve to illustrate this:

1. All record books must be kept reasonably clean and dry and protected

from the weather.

2. All books must be handed in to the supervisor every evening unless other instructions are given.
3. All entries must be made on the site, legibly and in ink, and not roughed out and filled in neatly at a later date. Pages must not be torn out of the books, but wrong entries or mistakes should be cancelled and reference made to the correction if it does not follow immediately.
4. All features to be removed during excavation must first be carefully drawn to scale in the book and precise relationships or depths from a known datum given.
5. Descriptions of layers should take the following form:
   a. Position of layer and its relationship to previous layers.
   b. Its main characteristic in content, texture, colour etc.
   c. List of artifacts; in particular building materials should be identified and listed.
6. A space of five lines must be left between each description.

The space left at the end of each description is to allow for the insertion of comments on the pottery and other datable finds. The description of building materials applies particularly to Roman sites where there is usually an abundance of such material. It may be important to be able to place the use of certain materials chronologically and it is thus useful to be able to identify the types of tile, for example, distinguishing the different roof tiles from those used for heating or in bath houses; types of mortar and building stones may also be significant. So much of this kind of material is found that it is impossible to keep all of it and the majority is thrown away, only unusual fragments being kept once a record has been made of the various types and an indication of their qualities noted. Several pages must be left blank at the end of each record book for indices of layers and features with full cross-references. It is useful to be able to paste into record books photographs of features and structures at different stages of the excavation so that reference can be made to the layers associated with them. The easiest way to achieve this is with a Polaroid camera, which gives an immediate print and avoids waiting for the usual photographic process.

Once it is decided that a new layer has been reached, an automatic routine should come into operation. New trays will be needed for the finds, each with a cardboard label bearing the new number written in waterproof Indian or other indelible ink. When the new layer has been sampled, its position and description can be entered and the list of artifacts added as they appear. It is good practice also to fix a label in the side of the trench or

D

area surface, so that a tally is kept of all the numbers, and these points of reference become important as new people come into the square and when the sections are drawn. The labels, also written in waterproof ink, are attached to 4-inch nails driven securely into the side of the trench, not at a junction of the layers but each into the middle of the layer it denotes. Similarly, features are also securely labelled.

Apart from the detailed recording of each area by the methods described above, or similar ones, there are the main plans. An overall plan of the whole site needs to be maintained as buildings are found and explored. This can be most expeditiously achieved by having a permanent set of survey points on the site. These should if possible be extensions of the grid set out round each area. Much will depend on the size and planning of the operation. If it is to proceed from year to year the main points need to be set firmly into the ground with wood or steel pegs embedded in concrete. There are practical difficulties if the area is under cultivation or if cattle or sheep graze there. Either the points must be fixed in hedgerows or against walls, or if in open grass made flush with the ground. The main problem is always that of finding one's pegs every year and careful notes ought to be made so that these points can be identified quickly and easily. This could be done by taking a series of bearings on a fixed point with a prismatic compass.

As features and parts of buildings are exposed so they are surveyed and drawn to appropriate scales, always bearing in mind the ultimate and vital need to demonstrate their relationships in the published report. With the more ephemeral types of prehistoric and medieval building far more drawings may be necessary as large areas are stripped. It has been found necessary in many cases to survey and draw accurately every stone appearing at the various levels.

As indicated above, the grid established over the site is essential for the detailed survey, especially if it is combined with a sequence of vertical photographs. Various methods have been used of raising the camera above the ground and taking photographs by means of a long cable trigger release. The best apparatus is the quadropod in the shape of a 10 or 15 ft pyramid made of aluminium. This is light enough to be easily moved about the site but sufficiently stable to withstand strong winds. Care has to be taken to ensure that the camera is properly fitted into a horizontal position in the apex of the quadropod. There are technical problems in this system and much depends on the housing of the camera. Some excavators prefer to take direct photographs and to see the target in the screen of the camera. It is possible to devise a tripod with a ladder and aluminium tubing clamped and bolted together. For both systems it is necessary to lay an outline square on the ground related to the surveying grid and to be able to make a carefully calculated relationship between the focal length of the lens and its height above the ground so that enlargements of the prints can be made to a predetermined scale. Any piece of equipment on these lines should be light enough to be lifted and carried about the site by two or three people. If the shots can be made to overlap, one has a sequence of stereo-pairs.

Prints are enlarged all precisely to the same scale, the edges trimmed off where distortion occurs and then the prints are glued together on a backing sheet to give a complete vertical picture of the area. The photographs can be mounted on a sheet or kept as separate prints. If there is an overlap they can be viewed as stereoscopic pairs and vertical relationships studied. The method creates an invaluable record but it is no substitute for a meticulous survey. This is the only way in which to study a complicated sequence of ephemeral structures. They have to be examined from all angles and it is in the plotting of these traces that relationships are established and archaeological interpretation begins. On a large-scale dig it may be necessary also to have a tower from which general pictures can be taken and from which the excavators can obtain a very useful view of the site. From a height of twenty feet, relationships between features and layers become more obvious than at ground level. Some excavators are content to lash together poles and ladders to achieve the same effects but they can be uncomfortable to use and positively dangerous. Nor is a high tower system very suitable for photographs, except with a very high-speed film and shutter.

Methods of excavation

The excavation proceeds with the careful removal of each layer in the reverse order of deposition and this is a purely practical matter which can be learnt only in the field. The tool used is the pointing trowel, the blade of which should not be more than 5 inches long. There are two actions, one using the point and the other the blade. In rapid work the point is pushed into the ground and the blade turned to loosen the material which is turned over, pottery and objects extracted and the spoil pushed into a pile. At frequent intervals it is necessary to examine the layer critically to see if there are any new features appearing. While one is prodding a layer with the point of the trowel such examination is not possible as one sees only loose disturbance. To clean off one uses the blade and scrapes away all the loose material to a clean, even, undisturbed surface. This operation starts from one side or corner and proceeds across the area in the same way as a floor is stained or painted. This area when cleaned should not be stepped or trodden on until examination is complete. If the material can be removed from the trench—with a shovel into a barrow this is the easiest method. A bucket may seem handier, but is in fact slower and more clumsy to use. In open stripping, it may be necessary to wheel the barrow along planks to avoid disturbing the surface under excavation.

Pits

Consideration must now be given to special features, the most common of which is the rubbish pit. It was common practice before the modern system of refuse disposal to bury obnoxious rubbish. One just dug a hole and rapidly filled it in again. In the Middle Ages, however, there seems to have been a practice of leaving large pits, sometimes stone-lined, open and attempting to burn the rubbish in them, and they are certainly very much larger than their predecessors. There is considerable variation in size and even purpose. There used to be an idea that people of Iron Age Britain actually lived in pits! This must have arisen out of the discovery of occupation debris and charcoal in these rubbish pits. But in this period their history is not quite so simple, as it seems clear that some of these holes in the ground had a purpose before they were filled with domestic rubbish. Some archaeologists maintain that they were for storing grain or meat and there is certainly occasional evidence that they were wicker-lined. When they became mouldy new holes were dug and the disused 'stores' became rubbish pits. It is equally possible that some Roman pits were for housing collection baskets or casks, where usable wastes were placed and later recovered. It is known that there was a Roman industry in collecting urine and this may have extended to other waste materials. In Roman forts there were rubbish bins sunk into the ground in the verandas of barrack blocks in the form of wicker baskets with lids, although only in exceptionally damp or dry conditions has the wickerwork survived to tell the whole story. Then there are of course latrine and sewage pits of all periods.

Pits when excavated are found to be holes in the ground of varying shapes and sizes, filled usually with clean material, and there is often little trace of the waste thrown into the bottom. They have other characteristics for, as in ditches, the sides and top edges tend to erode and the filling sinks, or the top edge is squeezed over by pressure from above. If the pits are below a clay or sandy floor, inside a building, the sinkage is often patched with similar material (fig. 9). The upper level of pits therefore consists of later patches and other loose material which has collected in the

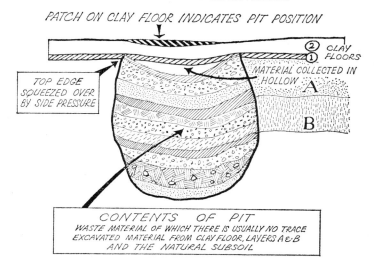

PATCH ON CLAY FLOOR INDICATES PIT POSITION

② CLAY
① FLOORS

MATERIAL COLLECTED IN HOLLOW

A

B

TOP EDGE SQUEEZED OVER BY SIDE PRESSURE

CONTENTS OF PIT
WASTE MATERIAL OF WHICH THERE IS USUALLY NO TRACE
EXCAVATED MATERIAL FROM CLAY FLOOR, LAYERS A & B
AND THE NATURAL SUBSOIL

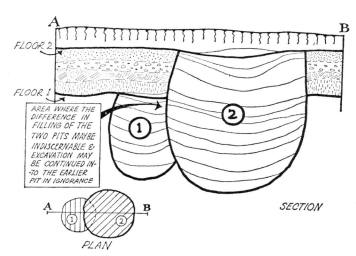

A   B

FLOOR 2

FLOOR 1

AREA WHERE THE DIFFERENCE IN FILLING OF THE TWO PITS MAYBE INDISCERNABLE & EXCAVATION MAY BE CONTINUED IN-TO THE EARLIER PIT IN IGNORANCE

①   ②

SECTION

A   B

①   ②

PLAN

Fig. 9 Rubbish pits: sections across rubbish pits. The lower
drawing shows one pit cutting into another.

hollows. Wherever possible pits should be sectioned and half taken away
at a time; if this is not possible for the whole of the pit, at least it should be
done for the upper sinkage layers as these may contain critical dating
sherds. The pottery from the pits themselves is very rarely contemporary
with the digging of them unless it happens to be with a load of rubbish
deposited at the same time. Pits often exist in groups cut into one another.

As their fillings are very similar it is difficult to separate them and one should be wary of the danger of following a pit filling to too great a depth, as it is possible that one is actually taking out the filling of an earlier pit, the presence of which is not immediately obvious (fig. 9). At the sides and bottom of a pit cut into sandy subsoil there may be an 'iron-pan' effect—this is a thin, hard, dark brown 'crust' caused by the precipitation of the constituents of iron compounds from the water which has percolated through organic material.[1]

STRUCTURAL FEATURES

Such is the infinite variety of building methods and materials that one would need several volumes to deal adequately with the archaeological problems it creates. In this very brief survey only some of the more common types will be considered and in particular their stratigraphical aspects.

Wells

Wells are very common on Roman and medieval sites.[2] They are difficult to excavate but in this very fact the challenge presented exercises a fascination for some people. Whether the results achieved from the excavation of wells are always commensurate with the great efforts put into them is often a matter of doubt. There are some good reasons for their excavation: 1. For the completion of one's work on the site; 2. They give important information about the relative levels of water tables in ancient and modern times; 3. The material which has been under water since the time the well was in use may include perishable objects in timber, leather and textiles which may have considerable interest and importance; 4. At the bottom one may find complete vessels of pottery or metal which had fallen off the rope used for drawing the water. They may help to date the period of use of the well and provide museum specimens; 5. At the bottom of the well there is usually organic material which collected during the time it was open. When submitted for scientific examination it can provide information about the ecology of the site, although it may require more than one scientist to work on the pollen grains, seed cases, botanical fragments, snail

[1] For this and similar problems one should consult I. W. Cornwall, *Soils for the Archaeologist*, 1948.

[2] For excavations of wells, see P. Corder and J. L. Kirk, *A Roman Villa at Langton, near Malton, E. Yorks* (1932), 49-55; P. Rahtz and L. G. Harris, 'The Temple Well and Other Buildings at Pagans Hill, Chew Stoke, N. Somerset', *Proc. Somerset Archaeol. and Natur. Hist. Soc.*, 101-102 (1956-1957), 15-51; Helen O'Neil, 'Building Construction in a Rural Area of Roman Britain', *Studies in Building History*, 1961, 34. For timber-lined wells see C. F. C. Hawkes and M. R. Hull, *Camulodunum* (1947), 126.

shells, insect remains and micro-organisms.[1] Very often, wells also produce substantial quantities of bones, perhaps in the form of complete skeletons, which are of special value to those studying the animals of the period.

The filling of the well will usually be found to have taken place in stages but the changes in material will not always be obvious to the excavator. It is therefore essential to log everything by the foot depth. Some wells are fairly shallow, being only 15 or 20 ft deep, and these present little trouble in excavating. When one has a well of 60 or 70 ft, however, special precautions are necessary and the task should not be contemplated without a stout and efficient windlass and pulley system, a good light and a crash helmet for the excavator and a strong pump to lower the water level. If the stone lining of the well is loose and in danger of collapse it can be secured by means of steel hoops. The hoops have a break in them and at this point the ends are turned inwards and drilled to take a screw. This enables them to be inserted against vertical planks and expanded by the turning of the screw until they are tight.

Timber buildings[2]

Until the industrial revolution there was always a plentiful supply of timber in this country and there were more buildings in this medium than in stone. In some periods such as the whole of prehistory and the early Middle Ages, almost all the buildings were timber. In the Roman and later Middle Ages stone was more widely used but varied in each locality according to its availability. Many stone foundations and footings must have carried timber superstructures and the practice of building half-timbered dwellings was widespread in Britain until bricks became so plentiful.

When a building has been destroyed or demolished only the parts below ground-level normally survive. Simple framed structures with their horizontal timbers, or sole plates, resting on the original ground level could

[1] G. R. Coope and P. J. Osborne, 'Report on the Coleopterous Fauna of the Roman Well at Barnsley Park, Glos', *Trans. Bristol and Glos. Archaeol. Soc.*, 86 (1967), 84-87.

[2] For a useful introduction to Roman military timber buildings see I. A. Richmond, 'Roman Timber Building', *Studies in Building History*, 1961, chap. 1. Details of timber-work in house construction are recorded from Verulamium by S. S. Frere in *Antiq. J.*, 39 (1959), pl. ii; 40 (1960), 8, and by Miss K. M. Richardson in *Archaeologia*, 90 (1944), 85. The effect produced by palisade slots can be seen in J. P. Bushe-Fox, *Fourth Report on the Excavations of the Roman Fort at Richborough, Kent* (1949), pls vi (a) and ix. For early medieval timber-work see B. Hope-Taylor, 'The Norman motte at Abinger, Surrey and its Wooden Castle', *Recent Archaeological Excavations in Britain* (1956), 223-249 and the full excavation report in *Archaeol. J.*, 107 (1952), 15-43.

therefore be removed, and if the site is subsequently ploughed no trace is left at all. This must have been the fate of thousands of ancient structures. Their presence is often suspected because there may be an enclosure ditch or a scatter of occupation debris, but if one scraped the whole site bare it is doubtful if the slightest hints of any building would be recovered. When there has been little or no ploughing it is possible to recover details of these structures by large scale stripping, careful excavation and close observation and recording.[1]

Post-holes

Fortunately there are other types of building where the structural members are sunk below ground. These may take the form of post-holes, and one is left working out plans of different kinds of buildings from a sequence of post-holes of varying characteristics. On some sites there are so many post-holes and pits that it is extremely difficult to form them into any coherent plan of structures.[2] Posts can be put into the ground either by being driven by a hammer or by being placed in a hole. As there is a limit to the length of posts to be driven, this method is usually restricted to boundary posts. Buildings need verticals of 10 ft or more and these have to be let into a hole in the ground. It seems to have been common practice for the hole to have been made wide enough for a man to stand in it to hold the post upright while someone else rammed the spoil round the base until it stood up on its own. Sometimes a bedding plate of stone or timber is put at the bottom of the hole and even a little box-like structure arranged like a socket to take the end of the post. The spoil, unlike that of a rubbish pit, is rammed back hard and there is little sinkage thereafter. The most simple building plan would consist of four posts, one at each corner, but many buildings are rectangular, about 12 or 15 ft wide and perhaps 30 or more feet long. Roman military work is quite distinctive for the post-pits are usually square and for main members, as in defensive structures, as much as 6 ft square. The posts were often placed in a corner and the filling rammed very hard indeed. The timbers themselves will of course have disappeared but dark filling will have replaced the wood and the precise shape of the timber preserved if they were not later disturbed.

It should be possible to determine the building's fate. It could have been left to rot away or the posts sawn off at ground level or even taken out of the ground. Traces should exist for the discerning eye to note and interpret

[1] Philip Barker, 'Some aspects of the excavation of timber buildings', *World Archaeol.*, 1.2 (1969), 220-235.
[2] As at South Cadbury. *Antiq. J.*, 49 (1969), figs 2 and 3.

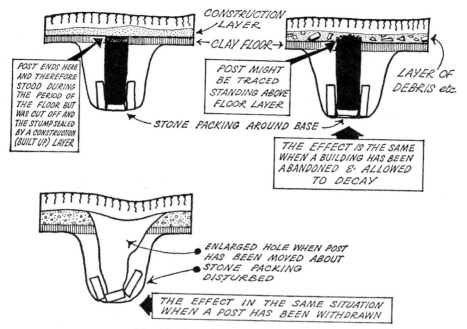

Fig. 10 Post holes and post-pits.

(fig. 10). Timber which has been removed will show in the disturbed nature of its socket in the original post-hole, whereas a stump which has just decayed away will still preserve its shape.

Another type of building construction in timber was the palisade or construction trench. A trench was dug along the line of the walls and upright posts set in it at intervals. The advantage of this method was that it was possible to align the posts more accurately than in a series of post-holes. Most Roman military buildings were constructed in this manner and occasionally it is possible to detect the positions of the uprights in the packing, by either the dark filling or areas of disturbance. Another method was to lay a horizontal beam in the subsoil and fit uprights into it. These beam slots are quite easy to trace in a light-coloured subsoil where careful trowelling will show the compressed remains of the beam as a slightly darker infill. If the building has been destroyed by fire the timber will often have been converted to charcoal and any clay baked hard, so that the structure will have been preserved and it will be possible to learn a great deal concerning the details of construction.

Stone foundations

When timbers are left to rest on the ground in Britain, the alternations of dryness and damp create the conditions favourable to fungus growth and serious timber decay. Evidence has been recovered from the Claudian fort at Hod Hill of replacement of foundation timbers and this must have happened very often. To counteract this, stone foundations were used so that the timber sill carrying the main structure was raised several feet above ground level. This is in fact the function of much of the stone-work on Roman sites, but it can only be proved if the actual sill is found. These stone walls are 18 inches to 2 ft in width and rarely faced with dressed masonry. The stones were either coursed rubble or pitched,[1] often herring-bone fashion, and the surfaces were later rendered with mortar or plastered to match the upper parts of the building. Much depends on the kind of stone and its availability. In the Cotswolds where limestone is very plentiful, one can today see farm buildings, several centuries old, which have stone walls 10 ft or more high on which rests a timber structure. When stone was scarce, a minimum height of about 2 ft would suffice. Walls of this character are usually constructed below ground level in trenches excavated to receive them.

Foundations vary considerably according to practice and locality. Roman military techniques usually demanded a foundation of rounded cobbles packed in stiff clay; other types consist of stones and lime mortar or the ancient equivalent of modern concrete. On the whole, Roman foundations are deeper and more massive than those of the Middle Ages—it is indeed surprising that some of our fine cathedrals have managed to stand all these centuries. The main reason for the depth of some of the medieval castle walls is the need to prevent them being undermined rather than secure stability. Roman public buildings like Fora and Baths had walls 4 to 6 ft thick, and their foundations went down 8 to 10 ft or more below the original ground level. The trenches cut for these were filled with foundation material and the rest of the spoil was then spread over the site, raising it by as much as 3 or 4 feet. Above the foundation there was sometimes coursed stone-work, still trench built, before the faced masonry began, and this is characterised by the masons' use of the trowel in striking the joints. It was Roman practice to start with good quality masonry well below ground level. Masons need room in which to lay the stones in regular courses and trenches of 3 to 4 ft in width have to be cut on each side of these walls. These are known as construction trenches and they were back-filled

---

[1] ie. set on edge vertically or at a slight angle.

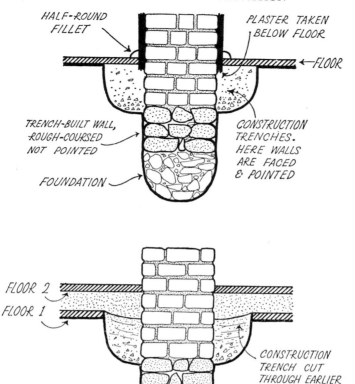

Fig. 11 Sections across walls showing construction methods:
walls of Roman public buildings in section, the lower drawing
showing the effect of a wall built on top of an earlier one.

with the material taken out originally, but they also contain masons'
chippings and lumps of mortar from the wall construction (fig. 11). These
trenches have a stratigraphical significance as they may produce pottery
contemporary with the period of construction, although most of it will be
from the earlier levels cut by the trenches.

Where there has been some reconstruction, it is necessary to give particular attention to the relationship of floors to walls and their construction
trenches (fig. 11). Even if the whole of the walls have been robbed away,

it may still be possible to assess their main characteristics from a study of the material left in the robber and construction trenches.

Robber trenches (fig. 6)

One of the most common features of ancient sites where there were stone buildings are the trenches cut by stone robbers who used the site as a stone quarry. Many of the Roman buildings, and especially the more substantial ones, must have stood for several centuries after there ceased to be any life in them. But when anyone wished to build a house or a church in the locality, a gang of men with carts would arrive, pull down some of the walls and remove the best of the stones. Large dressed stones and tiles were especially favoured. The great Norman church at St Albans, for example, was constructed largely of Roman tiles robbed from Verulamium across the river.[1] There are monkish accounts of this work going on and the results are to be seen in the Roman town wall, where to rob the precious tiles the workmen burrowed down and undermined this great structure.

The habits of stone robbers appear to be very strange in the haphazard way they seem to have gone about their business. Lengths of good walling appear to be overlooked, while some walls have had their actual foundations grubbed right out. The robbing often stops where the dressed stone-work ends, leaving foundations in position. Stone robbers probably took enough stones for their immediate purpose and tackled the handiest piece of structure, then when they had enough left the site. The only materials likely to go back into the trenches were the pieces of discarded walling such as lumps of mortar, plaster and unwanted stones. It seems likely that many of these trenches were left open and only filled gradually with erosion and vegetation. The filling is almost always dense black unless some building material was deliberately pushed back. Much of the final filling may have come about when the land was first brought under cultivation, and one often collects from these trenches great quantities of late fourth-century pottery from what were the latest levels on the site which have been in the course of time removed by the plough. These trenches have to be excavated first however deep they may go. Sometimes one is fortunate in recovering an odd sherd of medieval or even more recent pottery which may help to date the period of stone robbing.[2]

---

[1] This is well illustrated in the sections published in *Verulamium, A Belgic and two Roman Cities* (1936), by R. E. M. and T. V. Wheeler, in fig. 3, pls xx, xxi, lxxxii, lxxxvi, lxxxvii and lxxxviii.

[2] Martin Biddle and Birthe Kjølby-Biddle, 'Metres, areas and robbing', *World Archaeology* 1.2 (1969), 208-219.

Floors

Recognisable floor levels in a building can be very useful by their very definitive character. There is no mistaking a medieval floor comprised of decorated tiles, or a Roman mosaic pavement, but there are other types of flooring which are more difficult to recognise. One can only assume that in all periods there were many inhabitants who lived on straw and rushes or other organic materials which have perished without a trace. There is also the problem of boarded floors which must often have existed but are very difficult to trace. The most important characteristics of floors, apart from their stratigraphical relationship to walls, is the fact that the more solid types are often homogeneous and form an effective sealing layer. This enables one to clarify relationships of pits and other features which may rest on or intrude into them. When a floor abuts a wall it is obvious that the latter came first and either the two were contemporary or the floor may be a renewal. It is sometimes possible to trace several layers of flooring, one above the other, all connected to the same walls. However, where a floor has been cut by the construction trench of a wall, it must belong to an earlier building sequence (fig. 11). With substantial stone walls there is little difficulty in establishing these relationships, but in the case of timber buildings the walls themselves may have decayed completely and one is left in difficulty which only a close study of the stratigraphy can resolve. The materials used for flooring vary from beaten earth and clay, both of which may or may not be associated with timbers, or organic material such as straw, to a more solid kind such as concrete or stone slabs.

The detection of timber flooring is often difficult. One suspects it was there but how can this be proved? If loose planks had been laid down and eventually taken away, the only trace would be thin lines of fine material which had fallen through the cracks and are only detectable by meticulous excavation and observation. If the timbers had rotted *in situ* they may have left more in the form of dark streaks or iron panning. Where the boards have been constructed on joists, leaving an air space, and the whole left *in situ* one can sometimes reconstruct the arrangement by studying the positions of the nails which should be approximately in rows. The only indication of the presence of some buildings may be the finding of nails. If this is suspected it is good practice to plot all these finds and so define the areas of collapsed structures.

In the Roman and medieval periods there are solid stone or concrete floors, often built up in layers—foundation, cement and stone flags, tiling or mosaic. Even more substantial are the suspended floors in the Roman heating systems. Not all of these are associated with baths but more often form a method of central heating by the gentle flow of warmed air below the floor and by ducts up the walls, emerging at eaves level. To achieve this, a basement had to be constructed several feet below ground level, with a concrete floor to support the rows of columns which in turn held up the actual floor of the room. (Similar but more elaborate methods were used in bath-house construction,[1] but detailed consideration of these would take us beyond the scope of our present enquiry.) There are problems here for the excavator, however, as these structures, having been placed below the original ground level, often survive in much better condition than the superstructure. It is very necessary to have a considerable knowledge of these different types of system in order to interpret them.

One rarely finds a hypocaust system which has not been subject to alterations. Flues are found to have been deliberately blocked to raise or lower the efficiency of the system, whichever may have been required. Sometimes the whole structure was dismantled and the floors taken up and channels or sub-floor space filled in completely to support a new floor of a different kind. This may give the excavator a rare opportunity of collecting a fair amount of dating evidence from substantial levels in position. It may also involve the destruction of the later floors and if these happen to be fine mosaics there are the inevitable problems of recording and preservation. Modern excavation means destruction since it is only by taking the buildings apart that one can usually work out their history. Fortunately for us, excavators of the eighteenth and nineteenth centuries sometimes had qualms about this or thought always in terms of one-period buildings. They usually stripped down to the uppermost surviving structures and stopped. Many of these older excavations can therefore be redug by continuing below the floors and so revealing the earlier history of the buildings. On other sites, however, such as the forts in Northern Britain, the earlier excavators dug down to the most solid structure, ruining everything above in the process.

The most revealing sub-floor structures can be crypts and cellars. While these are common enough in medieval structures, they are all too rare on Roman sites. The filling of these spaces often gives the excavator a rich harvest of material on the date of destruction, but sometimes includes

---

[1] A brief, popular introduction to this subject was published by the writer in the *Cheshire Historian,* 9 and 10 (1959 and 1960) (published by the Cheshire Community Council). There is also a useful illustrated account by J. Ward, *Romano-British Buildings and Earthworks* (1911), 272-279. A study of exceptional interest where much of the structure has survived is J. B. Ward-Perkins and J. M. C. Toynbee, 'The Hunting Baths at Leptis Magna', *Archaeologia,* 93 (1939), 165-195.

earlier material. In some cases parts of the superstructure have fallen into the lower levels and these may be of value in reconstructing the building.

It is perhaps ironical that the more that survives of a building, the more difficult are the problems raised. One can begin to make an assessment of a building more readily when only foundations survive since the limited amount of structure allows only limited reconstruction. It is only when one begins to wrestle with the architectural and structural problems posed by the miraculous survival of the 'Old Work' at Wroxeter[1] and the Jewry Wall, Leicester, that one appreciates just how restrictive are the factors elsewhere. Yet the attempt must be made, for it is only when we start in imagination to put the roof on a building that we really begin to understand it. In Roman and medieval construction there are practical, structural and architectural factors to be considered. Here again knowledge and experience are of great importance. The medieval archaeologist has the enormous advantage of having many types of structure still standing in this country which he can study in complete detail. The Roman archaeologist is not so fortunate, and he has to travel to the neighbouring provinces in France, Germany and Spain to see buildings of his period surviving to roof level. Nor can the Romanist afford to be insular. The sooner he realises that Roman Britain is only a very small and not too significant part of a great empire, the sooner will he see his work in its proper perspective. Just as the prehistorian must always keep his eyes on the coast line of north-west Europe and its hinterland as the immediate source of most of his cultural associations, so the Romanist looks to Rome. With this constantly in the mind, he notes and assesses differences of building construction and methods and of planning in this part of the Roman Empire as distinct from another, and thus he moulds his own judgement.

Most of the examples considered above are taken from Romano-British archaeology, because the types of structure and methods of construction offer clearer definitions than in some other fields. Where buildings are more flimsy and ephemeral, greater difficulties may arise in interpretation.

One should never be stereotyped in one's techniques. Each site presents its own peculiar problems and one must meet the new challenge with flexibility and be prepared to experiment with new ideas wherever necessary. We are all conditioned and inhibited by our upbringing and in excavation we tend to expect our discoveries to follow a pattern already established in our mind from previous experience. The most difficult problem which every excavator has to overcome is the mental effort of the rapid

[1] *Antiq. J.*, 46 (1966), 229-239.

appreciation of the full implications of a new discovery. The more we know the less easy it is for a new idea to take root in the mind, and when a firmly held conviction is in danger of being overthrown we tend to reject the evidence subconsciously. It is equally dangerous to have a mind like a weathercock, shifting with each breeze and attempting to fit everything into an immediate pattern which soon becomes a meaningless array of disjointed fragments. If one is aware of these dangers they can be forestalled. Our ideas and experience must be allowed their weight, but we must always be suspicious of the suppression of new evidence or an attempt to change it to fit our preconceptions.[1] One's best aid is always the candid friend who asks the awkward questions and launches our minds willy-nilly into new channels. One has also to learn not to apply oneself to serious thinking too soon. Much unprofitable thought can go into a few scraps of evidence which happen to appear at an early stage. One waits until firm evidence begins to emerge before seeking to establish a pattern.

The work requires a trained and disciplined mind which can move smoothly and logically on its task of absorbing new facts as they appear But it needs to be a sensitive and suspicious instrument too, forever probing and looking round the corner, testing and sifting all the time while the full meaning is quietly digested and the measure of readjustment, in the face of all previous knowledge, clearly understood. The really important point to appreciate is that all this must be done on the site when the evidence can be seen and not later when one has to rely on one's own selection of photographs, drawings and ever-dimming memory.

[1] The archaeologist would do well to read W. I. B. Beveridge, *The Art of Scientific Investigation* (1961, now published as a Mercury paperback).

4. Scientific examination and classification of finds and samples

Introduction

It is very difficult to advise the beginner on the many scientific problems which accumulate as an excavation proceeds.[1] With the growth of knowledge and experience the excavator begins to understand the limitations under which he works. He must never forget that one of the main purposes of the excavation is to understand as fully as possible the environment and living conditions of the people under investigation. Ideally a team of scientists should work hand in hand with the excavators seeking the means to provide this vital evidence. Unfortunately teams of scientists willing and able to come to the beck and call of the archaeologist do not exist. There are, here and there, men and women skilled in specialist scientific and technical disciplines, who are prepared to carry out a reasonable amount of work if their interest can be aroused. The problem for the complete beginner is to find these people and approach them in the right way. The great advantage of belonging to a university with its many departments and its sympathetic attitude to research is obvious, but most amateurs are outside such an organisation and have very little contact with them.

With the tremendous growth of archaeology of recent years it would be difficult to publish a list of scientists willing to undertake detailed analysis and research on archaeological problems. Instead the CBA has a very valuable *Handbook of Scientific Archaeology and Evidence for Archaeologists* which indicates the present state of knowledge on particular aspects, with

[1] A useful up-to-date introduction is M. S. Tite, *Methods of Physical Examination in Archaeology* (Seminar Press, 1973); but for a salutary warning read 'An open letter to archaeologists' by D. G. Wilson, *Antiquity* 47 (1973) 264-268.

a bibliography. Advice is also given on the preservation of material if it is to be passed on for scientific study. The archaeologist should attempt to familiarise himself with the latest scientific progress in this subject. Most of this has been summarised in that extremely valuable collection *Science in Archaeology* (ed. D. Brothwell and E. Higgs, 2nd edn 1969) which will doubtless be kept up to date with further revised editions even though the pace of research seems to be quickening. If the excavator is fortunate enough to know a scientist who is prepared to help with his specialist knowledge, he should consider himself fortunate and try not to abuse this privilege. The more the scientist knows about the excavation and precise context of the sample, the better he will be able to assist. Better still if he can visit the site and discuss the particular problem with the excavator. The answer may well be that whatever he did it would be impossible to provide the kind of information the excavator wants.

Few if any of these kinds of problems are likely to arise on small-scale investigations unless they are specifically aimed at tile or pottery kilns or metal workers' hearths or smelting furnaces. The rather condensed notes below are to be taken as a guide to some of the phenomena which may be present on a site but it is hardly to be expected that the excavator will wish to test them all at once. In the selection of items for further study he should exercise a little common sense and take advice from more experienced colleagues rather than involve scientists in efforts which may well be wasted.

The main task of the excavator is that of reconstructing the past and he must try to use every possible means. There is an important branch of the subject known as environmental archaeology. In this field the actual physical conditions such as climate, fauna and flora of particular periods are studied and for this purpose the most suitable deposits are old land surfaces and peat, damp and water-logged conditions in ditches and pits, lake or cave sediments. Evidence for these can be found in the form of animal bones and remains of vegetation including seeds and pollen grains. The bones may give some indication of the fauna and the seeds and pollen some indication of the flora. Pollen grains are virtually indestructible and can be identified by their shape when seen through a microscope. They are difficult to separate from other material, which has to be broken down by chemical and physical processes. A count is taken of the different kinds of plants and due allowance made for the fact that some plants such as hazel carry much more pollen than others. This study reveals the changes caused by forest clearance and the introduction of cereal crops by man and enables the flora at various periods of the immediate and remote past to be assessed together with the climatic changes which have taken place.[1]

Soils

The study of soils, known as pedology, can be an important ancillary to archaeology.[2] Humus is the organic vegetable matter below the turf or on the surface of a ploughed field and it may come as a surprise to the beginner to know that there are at least seventeen different forms. The main agencies in the formation of soils are the natural weathering forces which break down the rock into smaller and smaller fragments, the growth and decay of plants, and the activities of the small animals and insects and micro-organisms. The soil, especially the upper levels, is full of the animals, of whom the most important is the humble earthworm. The activities of this creature were studied by Charles Darwin and his report[3] is worthy of study by all excavators if they are ever to understand fully the uppermost levels on their sites. In the course of time the combined action of worms and vegetable growth buries stones and pieces of tile and pottery below the humus level.[4] This is most noticeable in sections where a distinct layer of small stones and similar material can often be noticed.

The excavator often wishes to identify old buried land surfaces or turf-lines in ditches, indicating the period at which the ditch profile was static. Such layers are usually dark grey with streaks of white where leaching has occurred. If there is uncertainty, the old humus layer can usually be discovered by chemical tests which involve the calculation of the pH value or Hydrogen-ion concentration. As this is a method of comparison, it is necessary to take samples of all the layers above and below the suspected humus.[5] The samples taken need not be very large—about $\frac{1}{2}$ lb is ample. The section should be carefully cleaned first and the samples cut and put into suitable containers. Ordinary paper bags are useless as the damp nature of the sample will soon cause the bag to disintegrate, nor is a polythene bag very good for damp material as organic growth may be induced if the bag is sealed down. Wooden boxes or glass bottles are probably the best containers. All samples must be fully and permanently labelled on the

[1] Geoffrey Dimbleby, *Plants and Archaeology* (1967) and Peter J. Ucko and G. W. Dimbleby (eds), *The Domestication and Exploitation of Plants and Animals* (1969).

[2] An excellent introduction is I. W. Cornwall, *Soils for the Archaeologist* (1958).

[3] *The Formation of Vegetable Mould through the Action of Worms* (1881), re-issued 1945, under the title *Humus and Earthworms*.

[4] *Antiquity*, 31 (1957), 219-233; 35 (1961), 235.

[5] For examples of the methods and results see *Proc. Dorset Natur. Hist. and Archaeol. Soc.*, 76 (1954), 39-50, and *Yorks Arch. J.*, 38 (1955), 425-445.

outside of the container: sticky-backed labels should be sealed down with sellotape or something similar, or well secured tie-on labels are equally as good. In this as in other matters, there is a need for closer collaboration with the soil-scientist on the site so that these problems can be clearly understood and useless sampling avoided.

Shells and bones

Shells of snails are good indications of the conditions under which a deposit was laid: whether, for example, it was in peat or stagnant or fresh water.[1] With other mollusca they are useful when considering the state of ditches or streams at given periods.[2] They may also contribute evidence of diet, industry and, as amulets, have religious significance. But one of the worst headaches is the quantity of animal and bird bones found on most occupation sites. A careful study of these bones will add considerably to the reconstruction being attempted, since these remains should reveal much about the diet of the inhabitants and, if securely stratified, their diet at different periods. If one can detect such a change in diet one should seek reasons for this. Much information can also be obtained about the animals themselves and the changes that may have taken place in their physical development through domestication. The story will, however, rarely be complete as very small bones do not often survive and it is only under exceptional conditions that, for example, one recovers fish bones or egg-shells.

The identification of bones is not difficult and any competent amateur can master this technique with practice and application and with the aid of good diagrams[3] or a series of classified specimens. The vast majority of animals encountered will be ox, pig and sheep with the occasional horse and goat and wild animals such as deer. An excavation report can be loaded with long lists of the animals and their bones, but does this really add anything to our existing knowledge? It should be possible with more expert knowledge to retrieve more information. On the other hand for the expert to attempt a detailed analysis without any reference to the excavator or the problems of the site is asking too much, and the same remarks may

[1] J. G. Evans, *Land Snails in Archaeology* (Seminar Press, 1972).

[2] Examples of this kind of evidence from Roman levels at Cirencester: *Antiq. J.,* 41 (1961), 69; *Trans. Bristol & Glos Archaeol. Soc.,* 78 (1959), 84.

[3] A useful start here is I. W. Cornwall's *Bones for the Archaeologist* (1956), where the excavator is especially referred to chapter 16, Study and Interpretation; also M. L. Ryder, *Animal Bones in Archaeology* (1969); Raymond E. Chaplin, *The Study of Animal Bones from Archaeological Sites* (1972); E. Schmid, *Atlas of Animal Bones* (Elsevier, 1972).

apply here as to those above on other scientists. Apart from the possibilities of a change of diet, one would like to know something about the age of the animals, when they were slaughtered, any special parts of the body preferred, the type of butchery practiced and the number of individual animals. There is also the possibility of disease and injury which may have affected the bones. The presence of cats and dogs as well as small mammals may add considerable interest.[1]

It should be obvious from this that the excavator must regard his bones as sources of potential information and not just more packages for the expert. It is almost useless to keep unstratified bones as they can hardly add anything to the story, nor can there be much statistical analysis if there are only a few bones scattered in different levels. The excavator is therefore advised to attempt to limit his problems and the labour of his specialist by a careful selection of bones. It is possible that an odd bone may have some special significance, and if there is someone on the site knowledgeable enough to detect this he should look at all the bones before any are discarded. Where useful quantities in pits or occupation levels are found, they should all be kept and carefully cleaned, especially fragile pieces, and thoroughly dried before marking. Fish and bird bones often present more difficult problems in identification as experts in these fields are not so common.

Occasionally there will be special deposits which need closer examination. Wells may produce complete animal skeletons of some unfortunate beast which has fallen in. On temple sites there may be ritual deposits of sacrificial victims indicating details of these practices, like those described in the 1936 Verulamium report from the Triangular Temple.[2] In the same report there is also a description of an interesting collection of bones of parts of five horses which were deemed to have been the waste products of a sausage factory.[3] These unusual deposits need special treatment not only in study but also in the field, where it is very important to record all the information about the relative positions of the bones. Only then can it be decided if complete limbs were buried and how much dissection had taken place.

---

[1] It is sad to note that in Britain, animal archaeology is still much in its infancy; there are very few workers in this field and little is available for research funds. The best work has been done in other countries like Holland, Poland and Russia.

[2] R. E. M. and T. V. Wheeler, *Verulamium, A Belgic and two Roman Cities* (1936), 116-119; another example is the deposit from the Mithraeum at Carrawburgh, *Archaeol. Aeliana*, 4th series, 29 (1951), 91.

[3] These remains were studied *in situ* by the expert who made the report (p 19).

Considerations of this kind are also very important in the case of human remains. The skeletons need to be very carefully excavated using the lightest of equipment—small brush and trowel—so that the bones stand clear of the earth and can be photographed and drawn. All the bones of each individual can then be collected together for subsequent study.[1] The kind of detailed information which can be obtained from a thorough examination of cemetery groups can be seen from the Royal Commission Volume on Roman York.[2] Prehistoric burials and ritual sacrifices of later periods sometimes demonstrate to the trained eye features which illuminate these practices. An example of this is the Neolithic burial at Maiden Castle:[3] the victim was decapitated and thoroughly dismembered, and a hole made in the skull for the extraction of the brain. The same report also includes a study of the Iron Age warriors who fell during the assault of the fortress by the Second Legion at the time of the Roman Conquest. The brutal savagery of the Roman soldiers is clearly shown by the way the bones, in particular the skulls, have been hacked about, even after death.[4] Careful expert examinations of skeletal remains can produce direct evidence about ancient peoples, their anatomical characteristics, age at death, physical injuries and abnormalities and diet, as well as any barbaric practices in the name of war or religion:[5] even cremated remains can yield useful results.[6]

Perishable materials

Subsoil conditions in Britain, with alternation of wetness and dryness, are unfavourable for the preservation of organic material like leather, textiles and wood except under special circumstances, the most important of which is in stagnant water, oxygen being absent. In these abnormal conditions the processes of decay are often arrested and objects can be recovered in a surprising state of preservation. The best of these have been the human bodies, such as the famous Tollund man, recovered from the peat-bogs of Denmark.[7] These conditions only apply in Britain to deep wells, pits or

[1] D. R. Brothwell, *Digging up bones: the excavation, treatment and study of human skeletal remains* (1963, a British Museum publication).

[2] *Eburacum, Roman York* (1962). Report on the anatomical features by Professor Roger Warwick, 109-110.

[3] R. E. M. Wheeler, *Maiden Castle, Dorset* (1943), 344. Report by Dr G. M. Morant.

[4] *Ibid.*, 351-356. A fuller anatomical report appeared in *Biometrika*, 31 (1940), 295ff.

[5] Calvin Wells, *Bones, Bodies and Disease* (1964); and D. R. Brothwell, 'Cannibalism in Early Britain', *Antiquity*, 35 (1961), 304-307.

[6] Calvin Wells, 'A Study of Cremation', *Antiquity*, 34 (1960), 29-37.

[7] M. A. Cotton, 'Preservation in Iron Age Bog Burials', *Archaeol. N. L.*, 6 (1960), 247-251. P. V. Glob, *The Bog People* (1969, Paladin).

ditches on sites where the water-table has always been fairly high. From such levels it is possible to find pieces of wood and leather and, more rarely, textile.[1] The excavator must see that these objects are kept under water until they can reach a museum laboratory when they can be slowly dried and the water replaced by oil or carbowax. If premature drying takes place the objects will crack and warp and finally disintegrate. The same also applies to objects of shale, found as bracelets and pieces of furniture on late Iron Age and Roman sites. When these objects become dry they disintegrate along the lines of lamination. Another condition in which at least the form of the objects may be preserved is the burnt deposit. Wood becomes charcoal and the species of large pieces can be identified. Similarly seeds and nut kernels retain enough shape to permit classification. Thus burnt layers require careful excavation for the recovery of items as small as this, as they can add important details to the local ecology and the agricultural background.[2]

Some objects are too fragile when uncovered and it is necessary to harden them before they can be removed. They should first be isolated, allowed to dry (if this does not lead to disintegration) and cleaned as thoroughly as possible with a soft brush. An application is then made of polyvinyl acetate,[3] which dries very quickly, and the object can then be taken out in one piece and carefully packed in a strong cardboard or wooden box for transport to a laboratory. The pva can be dissolved by toluol and the object then subjected to leisurely treatment. It is often necessary to solidify objects or samples while they are still wet, and the pva can be made more effective by the addition of a wetting agent such as 'Teepol'.

Metal objects

Metal objects by their quantity, complexity and state of corrosion can provide many headaches for the excavator. From the late Iron Age iron objects become very common, but are usually in such an oxidised state that immediate identification is not possible. The oxides form layers and nodules which give little indication of the original shape of the object. Bronzes have

[1] An important introduction to the study of man-made objects is Henry Hodges, *Artifacts* (1964). See also R. Reed, *Ancient Skins, Parchments and Leathers* (1972).

[2] Grain and other seeds sometimes survive in a carbonised state and can be identified: Hans Helbaek, *Science in Archaeology*, 1969, 206-214. A destruction deposit from the Roman villa at Great Casterton, Rutland, produced seeds of cabbage (*brassica*) and a piece of knotted rope of flax, probably from a net. *The Roman Town and Villa at Great Casterton, Rutland* (1951), 19-20.

[3] This substance is usually obtained in crystal form and dissolved in toluol, 20 grs of pva to 100 ccs of toluol; emulsions such as Polybond etc. can also be obtained.

a green corrosion or patina and vary in their condition according to the alloys used and subsoil conditions. Lead tends to oxidise to a white powder, silver objects turn purple or black, while gold changes the least. The moment these objects are removed from the ground the processes of decay are accelerated. The ideal solution is to take all these objects direct to the museum where they are to be kept, and when they have been cleaned and treated, with the corrosions arrested and removed, they can be studied and drawn for publication. Very few museums, however, are equipped with either laboratories or skilled technical staff to deal with objects from excavations. The excavator is advised to discuss these problems with the curator of the museum where the objects will be housed and work out a suitable arrangement with him.

Most objects of bronze, lead, pewter, tin, silver and gold can be studied and drawn without treatment, although there may be details of decoration which are hidden below corrosion and will need to be added to the drawing later. Even so the excavator should not keep these objects any longer than necessary as, in the case of bronze, corrosion may take place rapidly with the formation of bright green areas; this is known as 'bronze disease'. The fine, smooth patina which forms on the surface of the bronze buried under the ground may only be a thin skin over chemical action which has reduced the core of the object to powder.[1] Bronzes with active corrosion should, as soon as possible, be taken to a museum to be treated with benzotrizole in a vacuum.[2]

Iron objects are perhaps the most difficult. If after the earth and loose corrosion is brushed away the objects still fail to reveal their true shape and function, they should be photographed by X-radiography.[3] The plates will show the original metal below the mass of corrosion. This may enable an identification to be attempted and possibly also a drawing; it will also show whether the object is worth cleaning by stripping away the oxides and other corrosion products. In many cases it will be found that there is scarcely any metal left. This treatment, which is often carried out in an electrolytic or ultrasonic tank,[4] should be left to those who are skilled and

---

[1] For a fuller understanding of this and other kinds of metal decay and their laboratory treatment see H. J. Plenderleith, *The Conservation of Antiquities and Works of Art* (1956), chap. xi.

[2] H. Brinch Madsen, 'A preliminary note on the use of benzotrizole for stabilising bronze objects', *Studies in Conservation,* 12.4 (1967), 163-166.

[3] For examples see the *Antiq. J.,* 38 (1958), pls 26 and 27.

[4] R. M. Organ, *Design for Scientific Conservation of Antiquities* (1968), 436-443.

experienced in these matters.[1] Roman and medieval sites often produce great quantities of nails and it becomes a problem as to how many to keep and illustrate. There should certainly be an attempt to collect a sufficient quantity to enable a selection to be made of the various types and sizes which can be classified and published in their groups.[2]

It should be appreciated that many pieces of metal are parts of composite objects, the remainder being in wood or some other material and identification is therefore not always straightforward. The amateur may need to submit some of his objects to someone who has specialist knowledge and he should be able to discover the names of these experts in various fields through the CBA Regional Group or from the London office if the local museum is unable to help.

Geology

Every excavator must sooner or later acquire some basic geological knowledge about the locality in which he is working and his site in particular. A clear understanding of the vagaries of the natural subsoil is essential in order to differentiate the disturbed from undisturbed areas. This has to be gained by experience and cannot be left to the casual visit of the geologist. But there are other problems which can be deferred until after the excavation. Where stone structures are involved it is useful to know where the stone originated; samples should be taken and identified. The use of special stones such as Purbeck marble and Bath-stone in the Roman and medieval times are examples.[3] On some Roman sites, like Colchester,[4] there are thin marble veneers from other parts of the Empire. There are also special stones such as whetstones, tablets for mixing ointments, Kimmeridge shale used for making furniture and bracelets etc. Accurate identification of all these is necessary and requires a specialist. The prehistorians have gained much useful knowledge from the study of the origins of the stone used for axes. This is done but cutting thin slices and grinding them down until light can be passed through and the crystalline structure of the material studied through a microscope. This branch of geology, implement

[1] A fine example of what can be discovered from a careful scientific study of an object is H. Maryon, 'A Sword of the Viking Period from the River Witham', *Antiq. J.*, 30 (1950), 175-179.

[2] An example of this is the paper by H. F. Cleere, 'Roman Domestic Ironwork, as illustrated by the Brading, Isle of Wight, Villa', *Bull. Inst. of Archaeol.*, 1: 1958 (1959), 55-74.

[3] W. S. Arkell, *Oxford Stone* (1947); E. M. Jope and G. C. Dunning, 'The Use of Blue Slate for Roofing in Medieval England', *Antiq. J.*, 34 (1954), 209-217.

[4] *Essex Archaeol. Soc. Trans.*, 25 (1955), 45-50.

petrology, has been organised by the CBA[1] and has led to the discovery of some of the main axe factories. Distribution maps of the finds of the finished products throw light on the trade routes of the period.

Tiles

The coming of the Roman Army introduced into Britain the art of tile-making and its use in building construction. The identification of the period and types is thus a matter of concern for many excavators. Although it is very often impossible to identify small fragments, when the piece is large enough or has a particular form it may yield useful information. Some examples of the various types of tiles found on Roman sites are illustrated (fig. 12). Mostly they are from the roof but the identification of pieces from a heated room or bath-house can be taken as evidence for the presence of one of these features. One must also watch for stamps on these tiles. Sometimes one finds the name of an army unit or the initials of a tile-maker or of a municipal organisation. A maker's stamp found recently at Alcester, Warwickshire, is only 2 cm long and 1 cm wide, and stamps so small can easily be missed, as also can scratched names or numerals which are by no means rare. No tile fragment should be discarded until they have been carefully examined. Decorated medieval floor tiles form an important group of artifacts for the period. Studies of both art form and production centres produce useful results in their respective fields.[2]

Slags and other metallurgical remains

Results of metal-working are often found on ancient sites in the form of smelting hearths, slag, crucibles, moulds and similar finds. These can be of great interest to a metallurgist and careful examination and analysis can reveal such things as the composition of the metal or its methods of manufacture etc, which may illuminate several aspects of the industry. Analysis of prehistoric bronze and copper tools, like their stone counterparts, can help to trace their origins and subsequent distribution by trade.[3] The method used has been to extract by drilling a small quantity of the metal which is ignited and its spectrum photographed by means of a

[1] See *Proc. Prehist. Soc.*, 7 (1941), 50-72; 13 (1947), 47-55; 17 (1951), 99-158; 159-167; 25 (1959), 135-143; 28 (1962), 209; 30 (1964), 39.

[2] See *Medieval Catalogue* published by the London Museum (1940), 229-253; Loyd Haberly, *Medieval English Pavingtiles* (1937).

[3] A very useful study for the archaeologist of this highly technical study is R. F. Tylecote, *Metallurgy in Archaeology* (1962).

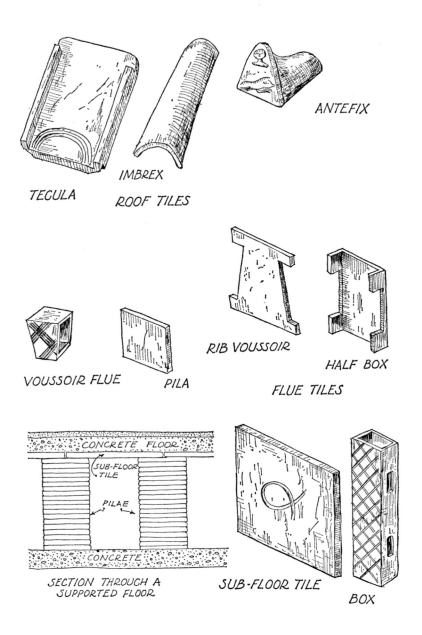

TEGULA

IMBREX

ROOF TILES

ANTEFIX

VOUSSOIR FLUE

PILA

RIB VOUSSOIR

HALF BOX

FLUE TILES

CONCRETE FLOOR

SUB-FLOOR TILE

PILAE

CONCRETE

SECTION THROUGH A
SUPPORTED FLOOR

SUB-FLOOR TILE

BOX

Fig. 12 Types of Roman tiles.

spectrometer. In one series of analyses,[1] 438 bronzes were subjected to this method. This brought to light the use of lead in the Late Bronze Age in bronzes to facilitate casting and working, although it would have impaired the strength of the metal. It has also been possible to suggest the presence of sub-groups with an excess or absence of some elements and work on a more extensive scale will enable the prehistorians to define close groups and trace the metals back to their ores. One of the difficult problems is the re-use of old bronze. The large number of smiths' hoards show that the precious metal was collected for remelting and casting into new forms.

Most excavations on Roman and post-Roman sites produce examples of slags, metal ores and similar remains, and it seems comparatively easy for the excavator to send them to a laboratory for expert examination. Lists of analyses in excavation reports are of little immediate value to anyone unless they can be shown to give evidence for methods of metal production or fashioning or information regarding the economy of the site.[2] In this, as in other matters, the important factor is the close collaboration between the excavator thinking in terms of site problems and the scientist and technician to whom a lump of slag may otherwise have no other meaning than that of an analysis chore.

Dating agencies

One of the most difficult tasks facing any excavator is that of dating his site from the sequence of events he uncovers. There may be striking differences between both cultures and periods. In dealing with the remote past in north-western Europe, the prehistorians may have very little in the form of material remains, perhaps only scraps of pottery. If this pottery has any characteristic form or decoration it may be possible to recognise a likeness to that from other sites. In this way a cultural sequence can be worked out and it may even be possible to establish the routes taken by wandering or migrating bands of peoples. But this does not help to give a date to the site in terms of absolute chronology. One might be able to say that it belongs to a period or culture but the dates affixed to these may be sheer guesswork. Just how speculative some of these have been is now becoming apparent from the discovery of a dating agent in the form of radio-active

[1] M. A. Smith and A. E. Blin-Stoyle, 'A Sample Analysis of British Middle and Late Bronze Age Materials using Optical Spectrometry', *Proc. Prehist. Soc.*, 25 (1959), 188-208.

[2] Useful reports are published in the *Bulletin of the Historical Metallurgy Group*, which has been issued regularly since 1963 by the Iron and Steel Institute, 4 Grosvenor Gardens, London SW1, for a modest subscription.

carbon ie. C14. Some of the carbon atoms are radio-active, and in the atmosphere and living matter the proportion of radio-active to ordinary atoms is constant and had been so for several thousand years until the widespread use of coal and the more recent nuclear disturbances, although scientists are not in full agreement over this point. The moment an organism dies and ceases to absorb carbon, the radio-active atoms decay and are never replaced. This rate of decay is steady and has been measured. In any piece of dead organism half the radio-active atoms will have become ordinary atoms in about 5,570 years.[1] There are various methods by which this can be measured and they are all very complicated and expensive, but the possibility of establishing an absolute chronology to any period or culture of the remote past has in the last thirty years revolutionised prehistory. The results have varied greatly and have in some cases been most surprising. More refined techniques are constantly being developed.[2] C14 determinations have been made for tree-ring sequences of the bristle-cone-pine (*pinus aristata*) which in the White Mountains of east-central California has a life of nearly 5,000 years. The circular rings can be counted and accurate absolute dates obtained. When these are compared with the C14 results taken from wood samples from the dated sequence, substantial discrepancies appear. These are due to the C14 content in the atmosphere not having been constant in the past. These comparisons have enabled a graph to be prepared from which adjustments can be made in terms of absolute chronology.[3] Radio-activity is of course common to other elements and it is possible that other methods will be evolved. At present its usefulness is limited to the more ancient periods, and sites occupied within the last two or three thousand years will not benefit from C14, since it is impossible with present methods to narrow the margin of dating to less than $\pm$ 100 years. This is too great a margin within the historic period when it is possible to arrive at more precise dating by other means.

Another method, based on radio-activity, is thermoluminescence dating. This can be used for artifacts composed of material in crystalline form and has particular application to pottery and glass. It is based on the collection of electrons in traps or defects in the crystal lattice. These free electrons are the result of the emissions of radio-active isotopes mainly of thorium, uranium and potassium in the soil in which the sherds are buried and also

[1] A more accurate determination is 5,730 $\pm$ 30, but for sake of comparability, results are adjusted to the 'old' half-life of 5,570.

[2] See Notes and News in recent numbers of *Antiquity* where an attempt is made to keep pace with new results for which there is now a special scientific periodical, *Radiocarbon*.

[3] *Antiquity,* 41 (1967), 266-270; 44 (1970), 38-45.

from within the pottery and glass itself. There is also a certain amount of cosmic radiation. The longer the sherd remains in the ground the greater the number of emissions which will be caught and held. This can be assessed by heating the particles of the sherd and measuring the amount of energy, in the form of light, released.[1] There are serious practical difficulties which are gradually being overcome[2] and it may be possible eventually to achieve a degree of accuracy of $\pm$ 5 per cent. One of the interesting achievements of this method is the certain detection of modern forgeries of ancient pottery and figurines.

At one time, it was considered that a useful means of establishing an absolute chronology would be by means of the study of tree-rings, known as dendrochronology. All trees form rings each year and they vary in thickness according to the weather conditions. While useful results have been obtained in America by Dr Douglas, it is doubtful whether such success will be obtained in Europe where the seasonal variations are not so clear. Furthermore, in some trees the same rings vary in thickness in different parts of their circumference; added to this are considerable practical difficulties in studying the rings on old beams and charred remains from ancient sites.[3] However, work is continuing on these problems and it is possible that some of the difficulties will be overcome. It is unfortunately rare in Britain that one obtains a piece of timber with a ring sequence long enough to enable it to be fitted to a predetermined curve.

Remanent magnetism

A technique has been developed for dating baked clay structures such as kilns, hearths and burnt clay walls if they have remained *in situ*.[4] This method is based on the behaviour of the iron particles in the clay when it is in a plastic state prior to its hardening during the process of firing or application of heat. At this critical stage the particles line themselves up to

[1] G. Kennedy and L. Knopff, 'Dating by Thermoluminescence', *Archaeology*, 13 (1960), 147-148.

[2] Progress is indicated in *Archaeometry*, 9 (1966), 155-173; 10 (1967), 26-28; 11 (1969), 99-104 and 109-114; 14 (1972), 257-268. See also McDougall (ed.), *Thermoluminescence of Geological Materials* (1968), ch. VII.

[3] For attempts in Britain see A. W. G. Lowther, *Archaeol. N.L.*, 11 (1949), 1-3; D. Justin Schove and A. W. G. Lowther, 'Tree Rings and Mediaeval Archaeology', *Medieval Archaeol.*, i for 1957 (1958), 78-95; A. W. G. Lowther, 'The Date of Timbers from the Spire of Chilcomb Church and from the Wreck in the River Hamble: some evidence from Dendrochronology', *Hants Fld Club and Archaeol. Soc.*, 17 (1951), 129-134.

[4] The theory and practice of this method is well described in M. J. Aitken's *Physics and Archaeology* (1961).

the magnetic lines of force in the earth's field and they remain in that alignment. This effect also intensifies the magnetic force and enables kilns and other baked clay structures, including hearths and possibly even floors burnt in a conflagration, to be located by a sensitive magneto-meter. The earth's field is constantly changing and the position of the earth's magnetic pole moves with it. These changes do not conform to any particu-lar pattern, and the history of the changes in the earth's magnetic field cannot be predetermined on the basis of known readings over the last four hundred years. If, however, curves of inclination and declination could be prepared for a known range of dates they could be used for dating, with reasonable accuracy, baked clay structures of the period covered by the curve.

Considerable progress has been made on this problem by Thellier in France[1] and later by Cambridge scientists[2] and more recently by the Laboratory for Archaeology and the History of Art at Oxford.[3] There are difficulties to be overcome, especially in sampling, which in the early methods was not sufficiently extensive. In some kilns, the fossil direction of magnetism varies in different parts of the kiln.[4] This may be due to move-ment of the structure under earth pressure or other factors which induce viscous magnetism during the period the structure lies buried in the ground. Methods are being developed to reduce this secondary effect, but the curves have to be constructed from our present knowledge of pottery dating. In a sense this produces a circular argument but sufficient is known of the dating of pottery in Britain of the period AD 50 to 250 to enable the graphs to be drawn with reasonable accuracy: it is the later periods for which there is some doubt. Sampling of medieval tile and pottery kilns will help to bridge the gap to the earliest recorded measurements in the seventeenth century but this will still leave a very awkward period between AD 400 and 800 when datable samples are very rare.[5]

[1] E. Thellier, 'Le champ magnétique terreste fossile', *Nucleus*, 7 (1966), 1-35.

[2] R. M. Cook and J. C. Belshé, 'Archaeomagnetism: a Preliminary Report on Britain', *Antiquity*, 32 (1958), 167-178.

[3] *Archaeometry*, 5 (1962), 1-27; 6 (1963), 76-80; 9 (1966), 187-199; 10 (1967), 129-135; 13 (1971), 83-86.

[4] This problem is discussed by M. R. Harold in *Archaeometry*, 3 (1960), 45-46, and G. H. Weaver in *Archaeometry*, 4 (1961), 23-28.

[5] The scientists at the Oxford laboratory (6 Keble Road, Oxford) are always interested to hear about the discovery of kilns and substantial hearths, as they may give them an opportunity of sending out a team to take samples for their research programme.

Pottery

In spite of all these new and exciting techniques, most excavators have to rely very largely on the scraps of pottery for their dating sequences. The making of pottery has been a craft through the ages, and potters have in general always been content to copy what has gone before.[1] The breaks in this consistent pattern are caused by the sudden introduction of new techniques or forms by immigrant potters or invading cultures. In a stable society unaffected by external forces, the pottery may remain almost unchanged for centuries. But slight variations creep in without the potters being aware of them. In a sequence of the same type of vessel these slight changes can be seen and they usually take the form of a smoothing out of details until some of the vessels become almost devoid of recognisable characteristics. Distinctive shapes and types of decoration often deteriorate with continuous repetition and the vessels become more and more degenerate. This process can be seen in prehistoric times when peoples were still wholly or partly migratory, and the impact of, or fusion with, other cultures became an important factor. The task of Neolithic and Bronze Age specialists is that of tracing the various cultural elements in the shapes and decoration of the vessels as well as assessing the rate of devolution.[2] In the Iron Age specialisation seems to have developed, as Dr D. D. S. Peacock has shown by means of the examination of thin slices of pottery under a microscope.[3] His work suggests that pottery produced in the Malvern area in the early Iron Age was traded over a large area of the West Midlands and further work of this nature may reveal similar distributions. Towards the end of this period migrations of Belgic tribes from northern France brought new and revolutionary methods into Britain.[4] Pottery with these new peoples was a highly specialised craft involving the searching for and selection and refining of suitable clays, the building of kilns and throwing vessels on a wheel. At all times previous to this, pottery making was probably a chore left to the women who dredged some mud from the nearest pond, fashioned the vessels into their traditional forms and left them to

[1] A. O. Shepard, *Ceramics for the Archaeologist* (1965).

[2] Examples of this work are I. H. Longworth, 'The Origins and Development of the Primary Series in the Collared Urn Tradition in England and Wales', *Proc. Prehist. Soc.*, 27 (1961), 263-306.

[3] 'A Petrological Study of certain Iron Age Pottery from Western England', *Proc. Prehist. Soc.*, 34 (1969), 414-426.

[4] Ann Birchall, 'The Aylesford-Swarling Culture: The Problem of the Belgae reconsidered', *Proc. Prehist. Soc.*, 31 (1965), 241-367.

bake by the hearth or a bonfire-type kiln which leaves very little archaeological trace.

The new potters were equally conservative but their technical skill enabled them to produce types suitable to the market rather than merely copying an old traditional form. The effect of this is seen in the coming of the Roman Army. The quartermasters needed a great quantity of domestic wares and the native British potters increased their production to meet this new and sudden demand and soon adapted themselves to the Army requirements. On forts in the south-west the local pottery was considered of sufficient quality and 70 to 80 per cent of the wares used by the soldiers were the product of local craft. The remainder of the pottery, the finer table wares, were imported from Gaul. In parts of the country where the local pottery was considered too inferior, the Army had to import it all, encourage potters from other areas to set up their workshops there or make the pottery in works depots with Army specialists. Thus a large amount of the better kinds of Iron Age pottery was in use after AD 43 and was only slowly superseded by new utilitarian wares of a general type. The detailed study of these processes in the different areas of England is one which has hardly yet begun to attract the attentions of the archaeologists. During the Roman period the vast bulk of material and the many different wares and forms of vessel make its study a very complex one which can for the most part only be successfully approached by systematic local studies. An exception to this is the pottery used by the Army. When the British and immigrant potters had established the industry the Army bought from any potter who managed to obtain a contract. Thus in a single fort at any point in the military zone it might be possible to find vessels drawn from many different parts of England. There is however a general tendency for the production centres to move towards the most profitable markets, presumably to reduce transport costs.[1] In the fourth century there were the extensive potteries in East Yorkshire[2] supplying the northern garrisons, which at an earlier period were drawing the wares from sources further south, such as the Colchester and Nene Valley centres.

The impact of new techniques, and the slow changes in the traditional forms and specialised marketing, are the main factors influencing the trends of the Roman period, but there are very great local variations. Much of the pottery travelled only a short distance from the maker to the con-

[1] This is clearly brought out in F. W. Walbank, *The Decline of the Roman Empire in the West* (1946), 31-32; a revised edition, *The Awful Revolution: the decline of the Roman Empire in the West,* 1969.
[2] P. Corder, *The Roman Pottery at Crambeck, Castle Howard* (1928).

sumer and this must be true to an even greater extent in the early part of the Middle Ages.

The archaeological problems of the period from AD 400-800 are intensified by the lack of datable pottery. There is little doubt that potters continued to work into the fifth century, although on a gradually reduced scale, as they were more restricted to local needs than hitherto; a few local and imported wares have been identified, and the list grows, but most of the local wares are at present indistinguishable from those of the late fourth century and there are no fifth century coins to date the pottery. The pagan Anglo-Saxons migrating from areas of north-west Europe, virtually untouched by any civilising or trade influence of Rome, continued to make cinerary urns in the prehistoric tradition.[1]

The full story of the survival and development of the industry into the early Middle Ages has yet to be recovered. The pottery of the Middle Ages is very largely local in character with some areas continuing in an earlier tradition much longer than others. But other factors were at work; the busy medieval ports like London, Bristol, Southampton and Chester were receiving the latest continental imports but these did not spread far inland.[2] The king and wealthy landowners could afford to buy and transport the finer wares as they travelled about the country or lived for short periods in their great castles. The factors which govern the distribution of many of the better wares are if anything more complex than those of the Roman period. The study of post-medieval pottery, at last subject to serious consideration,[3] is still in its infancy and can be expected to develop into a healthy growth throwing much light on one of the many aspects of the Industrial Revolution.[4] This brings us into a period of European world exploration and colonisation and it will be from these new areas of settle-

---

[1] J. N. L. Myres, *Anglo-Saxon Pottery and the Settlement of England* (1969).

[2] The pioneer of these studies is G. C. Dunning, 'A Contribution to Medieval Archaeology', *Rotterdam Papers* (1968), 35-58; This valuable work in tracing the continental sources of these imports has been continued by K. J. Barton, 'The Medieval Pottery of the Saintonge', *Archaeol. J.*, 120 (1964), 201-224; 'The Medieval Pottery of Paris', *Medieval Archaeol.*, 10 (1966), 59-73; 'Medieval Pottery at Rouen', *Archaeol. J.*, 122 (1966), 73-86; 'Anthropomorphic Decoration on Medieval Jugs; some regional variations, with special reference to Swedish examples', *Archaeologica Lundensia*, 3 (1968).

[3] eg. Bryan P. Blake, J. G. Hurst and L. H. Gant, 'Medieval and Later Pottery from Stockwell Street, Colchester', *Trans. Essex Arch. Soc.*, 1, 3rd series (1962), 1-11; J. G. Hurst and J. Golson, 'Excavations at St. Benedict's Gates, Norwich 1951 and 1953', *Norfolk Archaeol.*, 31 (1955), 4-110; see also papers in *Post-Medieval Archaeol.*, which began in 1967.

[4] See the *Journal of Ceramic History* and *Post-Medieval Archaeology*.

ment that we must expect information about the pottery exports of the sixteenth to eighteenth centuries. Already some of the finest archaeological work on this material is being done in America.[1]

These remarks have covered only some of the many factors which have controlled the development of the pottery industry from its humble origins. It is a subject of quite fascinating but enormous complexity and the excavator can hardly afford to neglect any aspect which may affect the sites of his particular period or type. Only by the careful study of stratified groups and associated finds, especially coins, can the archaeologist come to grips with these problems. But much can be learnt from handling the collections of local material in museums because it is essentially a local problem, but there must also be an acute awareness of factors which may have introduced intrusive elements.

Glass

Glass is fairly common on Roman sites, both as fragments of vessels and as window-glass, and the latter occurs also in large medieval buildings. Vessels become common once more from the sixteenth century onwards. The state of glass fragments is determined by the constituents of the glass itself and the subsoil conditions. Usually the surface has deteriorated and very thin iridescent flakes can be detached. Often on Roman glass these thin surfaces can be easily removed by washing; the fragment will be found to have been little changed and its shape and body can then be studied. It is rare that a piece is found large enough to make a drawing of the vessel worth while, but occasional Roman vessels show surface decoration in the form of engraved lines, facetting and trails of different colours. Fragments should certainly be submitted for expert examination[2] in case any piece is of sufficient importance for dating or for showing trade connections, and the more glass recovered and examined from closely dated deposits the more the authorities will be able to tell us about the history of the industry in Britain. The presence of window-glass should be recorded but it has to be very exceptional to be worthy of detailed study.[3] Medieval window-glass, because of its potash content, will be found to have disintegrated to a

---

[1] Published in USA, by the Smithsonian Institution, eg. John L. Cotter, *Archaeological Excavations at Jamestown, Virginia* (1958); C. Malcolm Watkins, *North Devon Pottery and its Export to America in the 17th century* (1960) and *The Cultural History of Marlborough, Virginia,* 1968; I. Noël Hume, *Excavations at Rosewall 1957-59* (1962).

[2] The CBA can supply names of experts who will deal with glass.

[3] See D. B. Harden, 'Domestic Window-glass: Roman, Saxon and Medieval', *Studies in Building History* (1961), 39-63.

far greater extent than Roman glass, but decorated glass if found in large enough pieces may be worth detailed study.

Painted plaster

Decorated wall plaster is fairly common in Roman town houses and country villas.[1] It presents serious problems for the excavator by its very bulk and condition. The decorated surface must be treated very carefully when cleaning and it is often sufficient merely to brush it lightly when dry; it can then be protected by an application of pva. Very occasionally whole walls have collapsed on to a floor and large areas of plaster can be recovered and constructed if sufficient care is taken.[2] Usually however the excavator has a number of isolated pieces, without much hope of bringing them together into a decorative scheme, but even here it is necessary to make the attempt and salvage what one can of the internal appearance of the building.[3] For the amateur this may represent serious problems in space and time.

Conclusion

It will now be evident that in dealing with all its bits and pieces the aftermath of an excavation can present the excavator with a few serious headaches unless he is assured of government facilities. If the project has been a large one and the finds numerous, it may be possible for a small team of volunteers to take on the work which interests them but there will be a limit to their knowledge and perhaps their patience. Experts who have made a life-study of particular types of artifacts will have to be called in and most of them are pleased to help as it brings them new material to add to their existing series. Advice here may be obtained from the local museum or direct from the CBA.

Where there are large collections of artifacts it is possible to carry out statistical analyses with the use of a computer. This is particularly applic-

[1] Most of the study of this material has been done by Miss Joan Liversidge. See her *Britain in the Roman Empire* (1968), 84-98 and 274-278; also her chapter in *The Roman Villa in Britain* (1969), 127-153.

[2] There have been excellent examples of this at Verulamium, *Antiq. J.*, 37 (1957), pl. v, 13-14 (this piece can now be seen in the British Museum); a piece of decorated ceiling, *Antiq. J.*, 39 (1959), pl. i, 17-18.

[3] The results of much time and patience on the part of Mr Cregoe Nicholson can be seen in the remarkable plaster from the Lullingstone Villa, G. W. Meates, *Lullingstone Roman Villa* (1955), chap. xii. Another pioneer in this field is Dr Norman Davey, who with government help has established a centre for the conservation of Roman plaster at Lacock and Pottern in Wiltshire. *Britannia*, 3 (1972), 251-268.

able to cultures such as those of the palaeolithic periods which are remote from historical records and whose development can only be judged from a study of their artifacts. This has led to the development of analytical techniques which most archaeologists brought up on traditional ideas find difficult to follow.[1] As these methods are refined there is little doubt that they will prove beneficial but at present it may be comforting to read a word of advice from the scientists themselves. 'Archaeologists are warned that although certain statistical techniques will provide useful tools to help them think clearly and arrive at sound judgments, these techniques will not automatically do all their thinking for them. The final onus of ensuring that their research is sound rests on the archaeologists themselves.'[2]

[1] The key work is D. L. Clarke, *Analytical Archaeology*, 1908; see also *Models in Archaeology*, 1972 edited by the same author.

[2] J. E. Kerrick and D. L. Clarke, 'Misuse and Errors of Culminative Percentage Frequency Graphs', *Proc. Prehist. Soc.*, 33 (1968), 69.

5. Publication[1]

There is much work to be done between the excavation and the writing of the report. The larger the scale of the work, the greater the bulk of the material to be processed. Before considering the end product, the report itself, some thought must be given to the stages leading to this point. Unless the excavation is a reasonably modest one or has produced very little in the way of portable finds it is almost impossible for the director to deal with all the finds himself. Help is needed in sorting and drawing. He will, however, need to complete all the plans and sections himself and the sooner this is done after the completion of the excavation or the season's work the better. The memory fades very quickly and the most important part of any report consists of the vital drawings which must be drawn when the details are fresh in the mind. The most difficult and often tedious part is known as 'phasing'; all the layers and features must be sorted out into the chronological sequence of the site. On a small-scale excavation the director normally does this as the work proceeds, although there may be problems to be considered at a later stage and even left over for further work. Where there are large areas, and especially under indirect supervision, the director has to rely heavily on the record books; one needs to make quite sure that all the entries are made with method and precision and above all are fully comprehensible to someone not conversant with the site. With large collections of finds it may be necessary to use tabulated sheets so that all the information can be entered systematically. First the numbers of layers and features are grouped together with the associated structures and placed in sequence. It is not possible at this point to begin to put dates to

[1] See also L. V. Grinsell et al, *The Preparation of Archaeological Reports,* 4th edn, 1974.

them. This is a more difficult and lengthy task involving a close study of all the artifacts. Coins and some classes of small objects may need to be sent away for specialist attention and this may cause delay. But the most formidable work is that of sorting out the pottery, unless one is dealing with periods or places where little was in use. The chief difficulty is to find the space to spread out all the sherds and begin to piece them together. Merely to examine each stratified deposit in isolation is not enough since very often sherds of the same vessels may be scattered through many layers. In order to be able to draw the pottery one needs as much of the profile of each vessel as possible. It is a mistake at this stage to begin to attempt to reconstruct a vessel with plaster since this makes it more difficult to draw it and in particular to measure the thickness. One should, however, where possible stick fragments together or mark them in such a way that they can be joined later. This would mean taking sherds from their layers and putting them into others. There is no harm here if all the pieces are marked with the layer numbers. One must always move sherds from later to earlier layers in this process. If, for example, there are three sherds found in different layers the vessels must originate from the earliest deposit or from an earlier one if all three sherds have been moved by disturbance into later deposits. Once this process is completed, one can study the sherds and begin to sort them out into various fabrics and decide which are the critical pieces for dating purposes (see p. 146 below).

'There are people who think they are doing good by digging and grubbing out antiquities, without making any record at all of their investigations . . . a discovery dates only from the time of the record of it, and not from the time of its being found in the soil'. Thus wrote the great Pitt-Rivers who published his own excavations on a scale which seems over-lavish by modern standards but which stands as a model and monument to his grasp of the logic of his work and attention to detail. He sought to record, he explains, everything 'however small and however common . . . common things are of more importance than particular things, because they are more prevalent'. General Pitt-Rivers, like many of the Victorians, thought in terms of an all-embracing universal knowledge which is seen reflected in the formation of societies for the study of philosophy, literature, natural sciences and the arts. The educated man was expected to take an interest in everything, the day of the specialist was yet to come. This is the spirit behind the great blue volumes he published at his own expense; his excavations were total and so was the presentation of the results with its relic tables and elaborate measurements of all that could be measured.

In his preface to the first volume, Pitt-Rivers states his reasons for adopting this method which, as he says, 'may be thought by some to have been made with unnecessary fullness. . . . Excavators, as a rule, only record the things that seem to them important at the time. . . . Every detail should, therefore, be recorded in the manner most conducive to facility of reference, and it ought to be at all times the chief object of an excavator to reduce his own personal equation to a minimum.'

There is a good deal of truth in this and such a complete presentation of the evidence enables a continuous review and reinterpretation so necessary as knowledge expands. With the addition of complete photographic coverage of the excavation at all stages, it might be considered that the General's pattern would be the ideal to which we must all aspire. Unfortunately this has become an impossibility simply on grounds of cost. Pitt-Rivers was a wealthy man and could afford not only to print the great volumes at his own expense but to present them to the new Carnegie Public Libraries which were at that time being created all over the country. This magnanimous and public-spirited action is quite beyond the resources of most modern excavators or the societies which support their work.

A selection of material is therefore highly necessary and in fact, with the steep rise in printing costs, editors of periodicals are forced to adopt a severe attitude towards the number of illustrations. Instead of echoing the General's dictum—this must be included for the sake of completeness—the cry today is: just how necessary is this plan or photograph? And by how many words can this description be cut?

Faced with an unpleasant series of choices the excavator must first of all consider most carefully what it is he is presenting, and to whom. To take the second problem first, must the writer of a report consider only the specialists like himself or merely the intelligent general reader? From numerous complaints from members of local societies faced with pages of completely unreadable material, it would seem that the tendency at present is towards the former attitude. There is however a very real need for a report to be, at least in part, intelligible and interesting to the general reader since all local societies depend for their continuity on the interested amateur with no specialist pretensions. This need can be met by a concise but readable account of the results of the work and a brief review of the wider implications. It has been the practice of Sir Mortimer Wheeler to insert this kind of passage at the front of his reports so that the general reader could grasp the full significance of the work before being plunged headlong into pages of closely written accounts of features and finds. Wheeler has always written in an exciting and convincing way, and one would wish sometimes that other excavators could emulate his superb clarity instead of sinking into a glutinous style which soon tires all but the most persevering reader.

The main body of the report should also be written with clarity and conciseness and in the third person, ie. instead of 'I saw that', 'It was seen that'. Its main purpose is the presentation of evidence to support the conclusions reached. The writer must therefore be conscious throughout of the results and not so much how they were achieved. To many amateurs the excitement is in the journey and not the destination. They tend to write an account of how the excavation was planned and carried out. The narrative is always the easiest and most natural way of writing and the writer must never assume that everyone else is just as interested in what happened as he is himself. The report may therefore start: 'We arrived on the site at 9 o'clock and the weather was warm and dry. Having shooed a number of cows away from the vital corner of the field, we started to dig a series of trenches etc.'

This is not the way to begin a serious account. The report should be arranged in a systematic way so that all sections follow logically after each other. It would be unwise to lay down any precise or rigid pattern as reports differ so widely in scope and content but a general outline arrangement may be suggested as follows:

1. Reasons for the excavation and a concise, intelligible account of the main results achieved.
2. A general description of the site, including the main geological and topographical features and a note of previous discoveries with full references.
3. Acknowledgements.
4. The main body of the report, which in many cases might be arranged on a chronological basis, the remains of each period being described in sequence. The chief structural elements should be considered first, followed by the dating evidence and any special finds, and if necessary with a section on interpretation.
5. Specialist reports which could not be reasonably contained in 4.
6. General conclusions, and a discussion of the wider implications when appropriate.[1]

These suggested sections will now be discussed in detail. The first section has already been mentioned above and should be specifically written for the general members of the public who wish to understand what

---

[1] A fine example of this arrangement on a large scale is J. R. C. Hamilton, *Excavations at Jarlshof, Shetland* (H M S O 1956).

125

F

it is all about. The topography of the site should be illustrated with a plan so that there is no need to give a verbal description of the position. It is necessary, however, to give some indication of the lie of the land, so that the site can be pictured in its natural setting with its relationship to other known features of the same period. The nature of the subsoil may also be important for determining the type of ecology and its bearing on agriculture. If the site were chosen for defence purposes, tactical considerations must be taken into account. When dealing with past discoveries it may only be necessary to refer to lists already published, as for example in the *VCH* volumes, bringing these up to date when necessary. (See also a note below on references, p. 129).

In the section on acknowledgements, the more important ones should appear in the text and lesser ones in a footnote. One may have to exercise some discretion here so as not to give any offence. Permission to excavate from the landowner and tenant should normally be placed in the text with suitable and gracious comments. Major help with loan of equipment and with supervision and special responsibilities can similarly be acknowledged here. It is not necessary to give a complete list of all the volunteers; if it is a small band they could be named in a footnote, and for a larger number a general acknowledgement will suffice, mentioning perhaps a few by name if they have been of particular service. These matters are very important for general public relations and any future work, and special thought must be given to avoid serious omissions. This is one of the ways in which the excavator can express his appreciation of the time and energy given, often freely, to him.

The shape of the report itself needs to be carefully considered before the writing begins. It is very easy to become enmeshed in a tangle of facts which may be clear in the writer's mind but, if not clearly isolated and related one to another, become meaningless to the reader who is seeing the situation for the first time. The method suggested is that of breaking the description down into the main periods, starting with the earliest. Always begin with the main features and proceed towards subsidiary ones. Wherever possible, reference must be given to a drawing or photograph where a relationship can be seen much more easily than in words. These illustrations are the real core of the report and the written account should merely give coherence to the whole. Methods of presentation of these illustrations will be considered below (p. 131).

Associated with each period there should be the dating evidence. It has been customary in past reports to treat all portable finds as a separate section but, unless these merit an expanded account which is not directly related to the site, these objects should be treated as evidence of the date and nature of the successive periods of occupation. Thus, unless the bulk of the material is small, the stratified groups should appear complete with coins, pottery and metal objects in direct association with the features to which they belong and not relegated *en masse* to the end of the report. It may be necessary to add a section on interpretation in order to demonstrate precisely how certain conclusions have been reached; this section might be more conveniently separated from the description of the features themselves.

It is very rare nowadays that an excavator is a specialist in all fields. He may find it necessary to ask other people to deal with some of the material. In the Roman field, for example, it is usual for a numismatist to identify the coins, and others to describe the samian pottery, mortaria stamps, brooches, glass, metallurgical and mineral remains, wood and plant specimens or bones. This may raise difficult problems for the beginner who does not always know where to turn for such assistance but advice can always be obtained from the CBA. These specialist reports will vary considerably in size and importance. If possible they should be inserted in their proper context with the dating material. This may perhaps mean that some may have to be split up so that the description of the samian sherds, for example, can appear in its appropriate group with the other pottery and objects. It should be made clear, with the first introduction of one of these reports or at the beginning under acknowledgements, who has been responsible for each section which is not the work of the writer of the main report.

Where the study of the object or specimen proves to be of singular importance in itself, the specialist report could be placed in a separate section. Examples of this are: the section on the Pewter Industry in the Camerton excavation report,[1] and the note on Relief-Patterned Flue-Tiles from the Forum Site in the Jewry Wall report.[2] On prehistoric sites these specialist reports often have a much greater relative importance and are often in the form of joint reports sharing the honours of authorship at the outset. Pollen and charcoal analyses can provide much information concerning the natural background of nomadic peoples when the remains of their occupation sites may be very sparse. When there is more settled occupation, as in the later periods, interest tends to shift to the structural problems. One of the difficulties with specialist reports is that they are

[1] W. J. Wedlake, *Excavations at Camerton, Somerset* (1958), 82-89.
[2] K. M. Kenyon, *Excavations at the Jewry Wall Site, Leicester* (1948), 275-278.

sometimes too long or obscure. They should not be cut or altered without proper consultation and this needs to be done with tact and discretion. Occasionally a short note on an object might be sent, or the information might be contained in a letter in an informal manner, in which case it should be redrafted, putting the observations into the third person and giving them a more formal character.

The final section should present the general conclusions and a discussion on the wider implications of the new evidence. Here it is necessary to hold oneself on a tight rein and avoid any fanciful speculation. Some archaeologists have a considerable gift of imagination and show little reluctance in using it freely. But there are others who feel that they must never allow themselves any licence at all in this direction, lest they be proved wrong by further discoveries. Surely there is somewhere between these extremes a sensible attitude where one can project one's thoughts towards the problems left unsolved or perhaps created. The excavator has a responsibility towards his colleagues and all his readers to indicate clearly the limitation of his conclusions and where and in what manner, in his view, further research may be required. Sensible archaeologists and historians are fully aware that the truth is not something one can dig out of the ground and document and enshrine as an absolutely unassailable fact. The past is a vast, intertwined network of delicate threads; some break or dissolve, but others can be followed and joined to other threads until one has a tiny, fragile fragment which may perhaps in the future join other fragments. It is inevitable that the more one finds, the more complex becomes the pattern of past events. It seems an easy and even inviting task to speculate on a few pieces of evidence, but the archaeologist must be humble enough in his report to acknowledge this, even if his work has to be inconclusive. It is, after all, only human to make mistakes and in assessing the value of fragments of evidence, it can be very difficult to preserve that delicate mental balance which produces an impeccable judgement.

All reports when they have reached a reasonably finished state should be sent to a colleague for candid opinion. Having by infinite labour produced a report, it can be painful to find one's brain-child so remorselessly butchered when it is returned. But this is an essential process and it is far better to clear up possible errors and misunderstandings before committing oneself irrevocably to print. Excavators are people with a natural feel for the earth and the problems buried in it; they are not usually as good with the pen. Writing to most of us is a wearying and laborious process and a severe discipline to be endured. One must be patient and painstaking and where necessary scrap and rewrite whole sections. The final version of the text for the printers should be typed on quarto sized sheets with double spacing and a good left-hand margin.

References

Particular care should always be taken over references to other publications in footnotes in the text. An approved standardisation of abbreviations of archaeological periodicals, based on a world list of scientific publications, is in use by the CBA in its annual publication, *The Archaeological Bibliography*,[1] and this should be followed. There are, however, some editors of county and local publications who still prefer the style to which they have always been accustomed. It is advisable for all those preparing reports for particular journals to seek editorial advice before proceeding too far, so avoiding unnecessary alteration. A problem arises when a society is in arrears with its annual publication, and a volume for the year 1968 may not be printed until say 1970. The publication is in effect the annual report of the society for a particular year. The practice as to which date appears on the spine of the volume varies and this may lead to confusion. The references should always be to the year of issue. The final reference is the page reference, which will specify the last and first pages of the passage being acknowledged. When articles are issued as offprints, perhaps for sale in a museum, the pages are sometimes renumbered to start at page one. If this practice is suspected, a check must be made in the volume to which the article belongs. These references should be constantly checked from draft to draft, for mistakes can be easily made in copying. Thus a typical reference may read A. H. A. Hogg, 'Pen Llystyn: A Roman fort and other remains', *Archaeol. J.*, 125 for 1968 (1969), 101-192. (Note the position of the commas and periods; punctuation should be fastidious.) Where the title of a book is quoted, the date of publication can be given with or without brackets; as as some books run to a number of editions, some of which may contain modifications that have affected the pagination, a careful check against the actual edition quoted is needed for page and figure references.

Where the references actually appear in the report will depend on the policy of the editor. The four possibilities are that they could appear in the text, in brackets, as footnotes, or all collected together at the end of the chapter. If the same reference is used several times it can, after the full statement, be abbreviated by stating 'hereafter referred to as Pen Llystyn'.

[1] A full list of periodicals, with their abbreviations, was published in the *Bibliography* for 1967 (1969).

In a large report with many references it is customary to publish a list at the front or rear of the article. Another method, the Harvard system, has found general favour. A full list of references is given at the end of each paper, with the abbreviated form which consists of the author's name (with initials after the name) and date of publication. Thus in our selected example, the full reference would appear at the end of the article and when a reference was needed in the text it would be given as (Hogg, A. H. A., 1969). The disadvantage of this system is that the source is not immediately identifiable since most excavators have many papers to their name. The system could be much improved if the abbreviations were those of the sites listed alphabetically, rather than of the authors.

The interim report

When an excavation lasting several seasons is planned, the problem arises as to when a report should be published. If the work is to be extensive and last ten or more years, the total results may be too large to be fitted into a periodical. When an excavation has been supported by funds from societies and individuals some kind of statement is desirable every year to keep people informed and interested. This need not be a very full report and indeed it may be unwise to commit oneself too much, bearing in mind the probability of conclusions being upset by the next season's work. There are several examples of annual reports which the student might well study. Professor S. S. Frere has published in the *Antiquaries Journal* brief accounts of his seasons' work at Verulamium from 1955 to 1960. These are admirably concise and omit detailed evidence which will eventually appear in the full report. (They are in fact written versions of the lectures Professor Frere gave to the Society of Antiquaries.) On the other hand, the excavations of the Roman town of Brough-on-Humber for 1934 to 1937[1] were reported each year in a much fuller manner. These reports are of special value to the student in illustrating the gradual development of an excavation and how new evidence appearing each year modifies the interpretation of the whole; one can see also how the excavators reacted to this changing situation. It means however that the early reports are valueless without the later ones, and one needs the complete set for a full understanding.

The high printing costs of today do not allow such a full annual exposition and it is now customary for a modest factual account to be written along the lines of the Verulamium reports even in the case of a large and

[1] Published by the East Riding Antiquarian Society, but reprinted as pamphlets by arrangement with the Hull University College Local History Committee.

costly excavation. Smaller excavations do not need this treatment and a brief statement in the society's proceedings may be all that is necessary. But the excavator should issue an account of some kind, duplicated if necessary, to all his volunteers. This is not only a duty but a help in maintaining interest and continued support. There is also the need to submit a brief survey of the season's results of Roman[1] and Medieval[2] sites to the two national journals for their annual accounts of discoveries. There must however soon come a time when a properly published interim report is desirable and only the excavator can really judge this. The criterion should be the amount and value of the conclusions firmly established, bearing in mind that much of this will not be repeated in subsequent reports. These instalments may thus be considered as parts of the final report. Perhaps one of the best examples of this process is the series of four reports on the Great Casterton excavations published by the University of Nottingham in 1951, 1954, 1961 and 1968, covering ten seasons' work. These four reports are complete in themselves with no repetition and contain little which requires amendment in the light of further knowledge. They are almost entirely devoid of speculation and both text and illustration have been subject to rigorous economy.

Illustrations[3]

Structures and features with their associated stratigraphical relationships are best demonstrated by drawings. The section and plan are the basic forms in which the evidence is represented and the report should be built round them. While the excavation is in progress the director must see in his mind's eye the final plans and sections as they will be needed in the report. Only in this way will the necessary work be carried out in the field. Nothing must be left to chance; before any part of the site is lost by back-filling a thorough check must be made of all records. These may seem unnecessarily full but there may always come an awkward moment when it is realised that a vital piece of plan or section or photograph has been overlooked. Nor is this something which must be done at the last moment; these vital records must be started at the outset and a careful assessment made of the

---

[1] The Roman Britain survey hitherto appeared in *J. Roman Stud.* but since 1970 has been transferred to *Britannia*. The editor is David R. Wilson, c/o Committee of Aerial Photography, 11 West Road, Cambridge CB3 9DP.

[2] The Medieval Britain survey appears in *Medieval Archaeology* and is edited by Professor David M. Wilson, University of London.

[3] A useful introduction is to be found in the articles in *Antiquity* by Stuart Piggott and Brian Hope-Taylor: 39 (1965), 165-176; 40 (1966), 107-113; 41 (1967), 181-189.

scales to be used in the different surveys, always bearing in mind the final report. As soon as the work in the field is complete, it is advisable to start on the finished drawings of all plans and the sections while the details are fresh in the mind. The writing of the text and study of dating material can be left to a later date, but where critical stratification is involved there should be an attempt at this stage to correlate the pottery groups with the section drawings by annotating the original field drawings or prints of the finished ones.

It is the usual practice to do these drawings on transparent paper or linen so that any number of prints can be taken by photographic or other chemical process at a reasonable cost. There are firms who specialize in this type of work for architects and surveyors in most large towns. The copies can be coloured and annotated for personal use, or sent to colleagues for comment or to volunteers with a duplicated report as a gesture of appreciation of their help. Tracing linen has the advantage of durability and does not tear as easily as paper. It is however much more costly and difficult to work on without experience. This material has largely been replaced by plastic sheets such as 'permatrace' or 'ethulon', their very great advantage being that they can be used out of doors in the rain and one is not at the mercy of the British weather when a critical plan or section needs to be drawn. Also one can make alterations with a razor blade, ink eraser or glass-fibre brush without damaging the working surface. There are different grades of tracing paper but cheap brands often sold by general stationers are a false economy as in time they tend to become discoloured and to crack. Reputable papers can be obtained from shops specialising in drawing-office supplies. Good quality Indian ink should also be used.

There are various methods of removing ink from paper and linen. The razor-blade or sharp knife should be used sparingly as these surfaces can be easily damaged, and when the ink is re-applied it may run. This can be prevented by smoothing the area down with a suitable hard tool. It is better, however, to restrict the use of these sharp edges to trimming and cleaning up the drawing. Much easier are the ink erasers of rubber or glass fibre. With the former one may have to rub away for a long time and care should be taken to pause occasionally and turn the rubber round to prevent any part becoming too hot and so smear the surface. One can also use process white to touch out here and there. On cartridge paper it is often easier to cut out small pieces of gummed paper and paste them over the mistakes and draw in correctly over them. The block-maker, when photographing the drawing, will pick out only black lines.

The selection of a suitable pen is very important. The old drawing-office

132

pen which needed constant refilling has now been superseded by a variety of new types which give lines of constant thickness and have ink reservoirs.[1]

Drawings, if they are not traced, should be done in black ink on white cartridge paper or very faint graph paper. These are eventually reproduced in the form of line blocks.[2] When the drawings are handed to the block-maker they will have on them precise instructions from the editor as to the amount of reduction needed to fit them on to the pages of the journal. Therefore, before considering the production of the final drawings for publication, it is very necessary to work out the degree of reduction as this will govern the size of the drawing and of all lettering, and the thicknesses of all lines and dots. A constant watch must be kept to see that the letters never become too small for the proposed reduction. Reduction also affects the drawn out scale, particularly its numerals. The scale of the drawing should not merely be stated but must be drawn out with alternating black and white rectangles in both imperial and metric scales, a rather more difficult operation than would appear, and needing great care and precision. Wherever possible an attempt should be made to fit the drawing into the page of the journal, as fold-outs are very expensive. Thus at the outset it should be possible to have an estimate of whether the plan or sections are to be reduced to a half or a quarter or any other fraction. Only then can one go ahead and plan the lettering and thickness of lines so that they will still appear legible on the final block. It must also be remembered that while it might be possible to remove something from a line block it is extremely difficult and costly to add or alter any detail. One should therefore be exceptionally careful to check all drawings for spelling mistakes and other details before sending them to the editor. In order to see how the drawings will eventually appear, it is possible to obtain a reducing glass which will show the image at half its normal size. Another method is to hold up the open journal and get someone else to hold up your illustration and back away until the two appear to you to be the same size.

Neat lettering is important in the general appearance of the drawing. One can obtain sets of stencils which give uniform letters and numbers of different types and sizes. These have to be used with care to avoid bad spacing and alignment. There are also available sets of stick-on letters and

[1] The best of these are the Rotring and the Koh-i-Noor designer pen both of which can be obtained with interchangeable heads.

[2] This is a zinc plate etched in an acid bath so that the areas and lines to be inked are in relief.

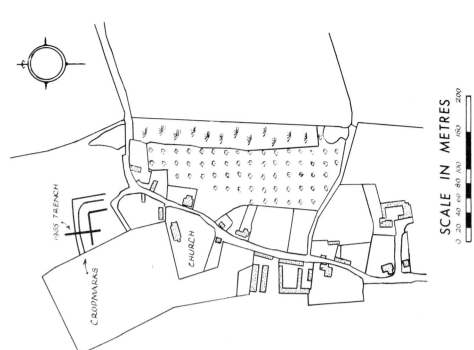

GRIMLEY, WORCS

SITE OF EXCAVATION 1955

CROPMARKS

1955 TRENCH

CHURCH

SCALE IN METRES

0 20 40 60 80 100   150   200

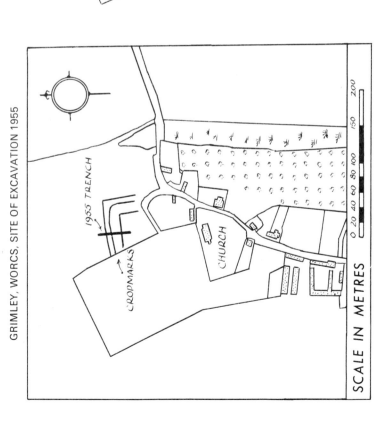

GRIMLEY, WORCS, SITE OF EXCAVATION 1955

CROPMARKS

1955 TRENCH

CHURCH

SCALE IN METRES

0 20 40 60 80 100   150   200

Fig. 13   The effect of using a border and avoiding large headings.

numbers.[1] The beginner should not however rely exclusively on these aids, but should learn to develop a simple and effective style of his own which in the end may be much easier, quicker and less expensive.

Drawings are sometimes improved by a plain-style line border and this should be planned to save as much space as possible and so cut down the cost of the block.[2] Nor is there any need for large and elaborate headings which take a great deal of time and use unnecessary space when the information can easily be placed in the caption (fig. 13). It is normally useful to put the initials of the persons responsible for the surveys and drawings and the date in the bottom right-hand corner, so that responsibility is properly carried. The reader will be considerably helped if all drawings are orientated in the same direction, and one is always surprised to find an occasional lack of care in this regard, and even a tendency to place the north point in the wrong direction. Over-large and fanciful designs for the north point should be avoided; it is better to work out a simple but effective type and adhere to it. Before despatching all the illustrations to the editor, it is advisable to retain copies either in the form of direct prints from tracings or photographs. If then the drawings are lost in the post or while in the editor's or printer's hands, it will not be necessary to redraw the whole batch. Reduced photographs are also very useful for establishing the permitted degree of reduction. It should be clear from this that a good deal of careful planning and thought must go into the final drawings.

Plans

A number of plans of different scales will be required for various purposes and these can be divided as follows:

1. A small-scale plan showing the site in relationship to modern features such as roads and villages. It has become a recent practice, especially among prehistorians, to place in a corner of this a very small scale plan of a recognisable part of the British Isles to show the location of the site. This is important for continental workers whose detailed knowledge of our country may not be adequate for the immediate placing of the site if only a small town or village is mentioned or if it is situated in an area of unrecognisable highland zone remote from any habitation. This practice is more necessary with national than with county publications. Normally the most useful scale for a plan showing the position of the site is that of 6 inches

---

[1] Among the best of these are the 'Letraset' sheets.

[2] The current (1973) price of line-blocks is about 1.5p per sq cm with a minimum charge of £2 for a minimum size of about 100 sq cm. There is therefore no point in making any block smaller than this.

to the mile. One can use Ordnance Survey maps for this purpose, providing authority is first obtained from the Controller, H.M. Stationery Office,[1] and this is stated in the caption.

2. A plan of the site showing the areas excavated and main features. The scale will clearly depend on the size of the site. It is necessary to avoid a large plan with detail which will not easily reduce and on a large site it may be better to have a plan which merely shows the areas excavated in relationship to each other and separate plans for each area with its features in detail.

Detailed plans and sections

3. Plans of selected detail should be chosen to illustrate special relationships between features where necessary. Sections can also be included under this heading, therefore, as they illustrate vertical relationships. Some types of investigation, as seen above, consist entirely of sections across linear features. These drawings therefore form the most important part of the report. Long sections present particular difficulties in reduction. It is not unusual to excavate a section 200 ft or more in length, and if this is drawn to a scale of a half inch to the foot, the actual drawing will be at least 8 ft 4 ins long. A reduction to a fifth would mean a block 20 ins long and a double fold. For the sake of economy serious consideration must be given to dividing such a long section into two parts, placing them one above the other; it is even possible with further adjustments and reductions to arrive at a block which would take a full page if mounted sideways and thereby save the considerable expense of a fold-out. When a section is so divided care must be taken to ensure that the join is not at a crucial point and that there is a clear overlap so that the reader can appreciate the nature of presentation. The task of drawing a section which is meaningful, accurate, simple to understand and capable of reduction is to the beginner a task of some magnitude.

The drawings done in the field will show, probably with the aid of colour, every detail of each deposit and feature. Now comes the task of tracing this in such a way that the relationship between layers and features is quite clear without the artist resorting to purely mechanical means of stippling. There are different schools of thought on this. Some attempt to show the section as nearly as possible as it appears to the eye. The best exponent of this type of drawing was Dr G. Bersu, and the results can be seen

---

[1] Application should first be made to the Director General of the Ordnance Survey, Southampton.

in his Little Woodbury excavation report,[1] and another excavator to adopt this style was Sir Ian Richmond.[2] Differences between deposits are shown by changes in the shading and stippling, varying in their intensity and angle. No hard lines appear at all except where there are stone walls and at the natural subsoil. This method has the virtue of honesty by omitting any clear-cut divisions which the excavator might suppose to be there without their being clearly visible. At the same time, unless one is extremely careful there is a tendency towards lack of clarity. A method in contrast to this is that of drawing clear-cut divisions between layers and shading or hatching them in a purely geometric notation.[3] While sections in this style are very clear and can be attractive in appearance, there is a danger in its subjectivity: one has only the excavator's interpretation of what was actually there.

It is suggested that a compromise between the best characteristics of each might produce the most acceptable result. Excellent examples of such a style can be seen in the publications of Sir Mortimer Wheeler, whose fine archaeological draughtsmanship has set a high standard.[4] This method has been followed by Professor S. S. Frere[5] (fig. 14) and Mr John Wacher.[6] It is a style which is particularly suited to Romano-British excavations where the stratification is normally clear cut. The notation should as far as possible show the deposits as they actually appeared. This cannot be done in all cases and with materials like clay and humus a simple kind of shading or hatching should be introduced which does not clash too violently with the rest of the drawing. No hard lines are shown unless they actually appeared. An additional but important refinement is the layer or deposit number as recorded during the excavation. It seems quite pointless for the excavator to introduce an entirely new set of numbers merely to put on the drawing. The numbers used should be those in the field records so that the actual sherds can be identified and re-examined at a later date by anyone wishing to reassess the results of the excavation. The deposit numbers are also needed for reference to groups of pottery and coins assembled for the dating purposes.

[1] *Proc. Prehist. Soc.*, 6 (1940), 30-111.

[2] As in the Newstead report, *Proc. Soc. Antiq. Scot.*, 84 for 1949-1950 (1952); *Hod Hill* 2 (1968), figs 16 and 38.

[3] An example of this is a section at Mancetter published in the *Trans. Birmingham Archaeol. Soc.*, 74 (1956), fig. 7.

[4] As seen in the Research Reports on *Verulamium* (1936), *Lydney Park* (1932) and *Stanwick* (1954).

[5] *Verulamium Excavations*, i (1972).

[6] *Antiq. J.*, 42 (1962), pl. vi.

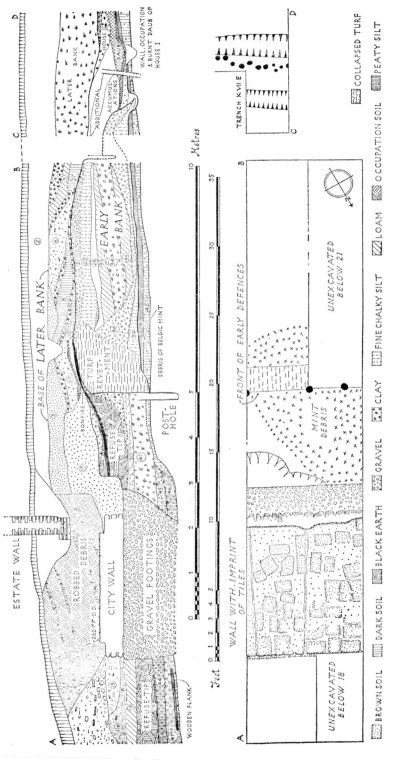

VERULAMIUM 1956: SECTION THROUGH NORTH-EAST DEFENCES

ESTATE WALL

CITY WALL

226.77 O.D.

ROBBED DEBRIS

GRAVEL FOOTINGS

WOODEN PLANK

REFUSE TIP

BASE OF LATER BANK

LATER BANK

ADDITIONAL ACCUMULATIONS

DAUB

WALL OCCUPATION & BURNT DAUB OF HOUSE I

HOUSE I

EARLY BANK

BONFIRE

TURF REVETMENT

REFUSE TIP

POST-HOLE

DEBRIS OF BELGIC MINT

WALL WITH IMPRINT OF TILES

TRENCH KVIIE

FRONT OF EARLY DEFENCES

MINT DEBRIS

UNEXCAVATED BELOW 21

UNEXCAVATED BELOW 18

Feet 0 1 2 3 4 5 10 15 20 25 30 35

0 1 2 3 4 5 Metres 10

BROWN SOIL   DARK SOIL   BLACK EARTH   GRAVEL   CLAY   FINE CHALKY SILT   LOAM   OCCUPATION SOIL   COLLAPSED TURF   PEATY SILT

Fig. 14 A section through the N.E. defences at Verulamium using a combination of shading and geometric hatching.

Illustrations have been prepared showing the same length of section drawn in the three methods described (fig. 16). Students should carefully examine different kinds of excavation report and decide for themselves which style suits their report and also their drawing abilities. One should aim at constant improvement and never be afraid to experiment and make mistakes even though it may mean much redrawing. It is far better to develop an individual style than to copy the notation of someone else in a slavish manner and without a full understanding of its implications.

It is important to indicate the main phases of building and occupation by lettering and it is possible also to clarify the different phases in the drawing itself. But this can be as dangerous as the use of hard lines and stylised shading if it imposes too readily on the reader the excavator's own interpretation, not exactly by suppressing but by glossing over details, the significance of which may have escaped the excavator. It is better to present the evidence as it is even if it is not clearly understood. Where a section requires an explanation which would be cumbersome in the text and would obscure the detail on the drawing itself, an outline interpretation might be considered, as in the example shown (fig. 15).

It is rare for both sides of the section to show exactly the same features and if each face produces different evidence it may be necessary to draw both sides.[1] It should be noted here that one side is then shown in reverse of the other, just as they would be seen in the trench. In this case a plan of the trench may also be needed to show features such as a post hole or pit which may not have appeared in both sections, or may even have been in the middle of the trench and not shown on either section.

The stratigraphy of a section is normally worked out as it is drawn and a clear understanding reached as to the precise relationship of all deposits and features. If this is properly done, there should be no need to leave either unnecessary voids in the section or produce stratigraphical absurdities. Examples of both of these kinds of mishap are shown (fig. 17) and they cannot be avoided if the excavator sets out merely to produce a mechanical drawing of certain features in relation to his trench. The section is incomplete if there are unexplained gaps and work must be continued until these are filled in.

Photographs

The excavator, if he is wise, will probably have taken a large number of photographs during the course of his excavation showing various features

[1] As in the case of the defences of Silchester, *Archaeologia*, 92 (1947), fig. 2 and pl. xxx.

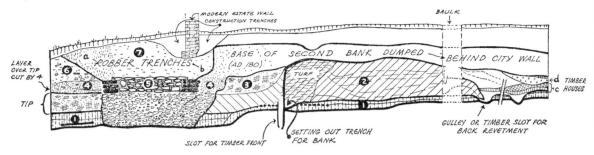

Fig. 15 Interpretation of the section at Verulamium.

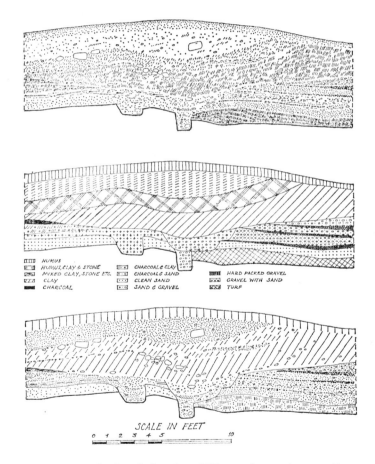

SCALE IN FEET

Fig. 16 Methods of showing different layers in a section:
from top realistic; stylised; compromise.

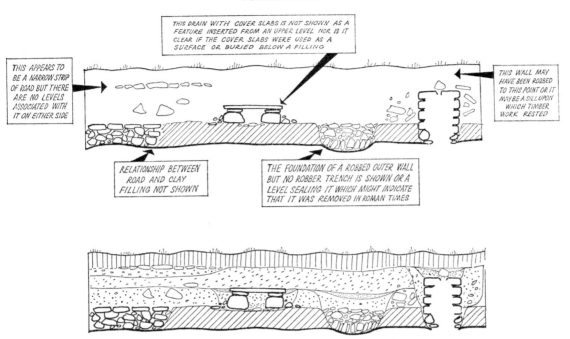

THIS DRAIN WITH COVER SLABS IS NOT SHOWN AS A FEATURE INSERTED FROM AN UPPER LEVEL NOR IS IT CLEAR IF THE COVER SLABS WERE USED AS A SURFACE OR BURIED BELOW A FILLING

THIS APPEARS TO BE A NARROW STRIP OF ROAD BUT THERE ARE NO LEVELS ASSOCIATED WITH IT ON EITHER SIDE

THIS WALL MAY HAVE BEEN ROBBED TO THIS POINT OR IT MAY BE A SILL UPON WHICH TIMBER WORK RESTED

RELATIONSHIP BETWEEN ROAD AND CLAY FILLING NOT SHOWN

THE FOUNDATION OF A ROBBED OUTER WALL BUT NO ROBBER TRENCH IS SHOWN OR A LEVEL SEALING IT WHICH MIGHT INDICATE THAT IT WAS REMOVED IN ROMAN TIMES

Fig. 17 Voids: *above* a section which shows features only without any layers which would establish their relationships and chronological sequence; *below* the completed section.

at different stages of the work. These are valuable records and a great help ultimately in arriving at a full understanding. But those for publication must be carefully selected. Photographs are reproduced as half-tone blocks[1] and usually cost about a third as much again per square centimetre as line blocks; also they have to be printed on special art paper. For the sake of economy therefore, it is necessary to be sparing of this type of illustration. One should limit these pictures to those which show features which cannot be easily described in the text or seen adequately in a drawing. General views, unless they show important features, should be avoided. Block-makers prefer to work from a good glossy enlargement.

[1] The half-tone block is made by projecting the photographic illustration through a glass screen with intersecting engraved lines. The effect is to produce on the block an evenly distributed number of dots of different sizes. On coarse screens, such as those used in newspapers, one can actually see the dots with the naked eye and the reproductions are correspondingly poor in quality. For high quality work the finer the screen (150 to 200 lines to the inch), the better the reproduction. But these quality blocks need to be printed on a smooth glazed art paper and not on the normal paper used for the text. Half-tone blocks cost, at present, about 2p per sq cm with a minimum charge of £3.

Having selected the photographs, the first task is to trim each one so that only the essential part of it is reproduced. This will also help to avoid extraneous features like heaps of spoil and tools which may have been left lying around. It is not necessary to cut the actual photographs down; it is sufficient to draw the outline on the back with precise instructions to the block-maker as to the reduction, but any writing or drawing must be done with a soft pencil as otherwise an impression will be left on the glossy side. As in the case of line-drawings, some forethought is necessary in arranging these plates. The photographs should be fitted into a page of the publication in the most economical way possible. It is not reasonable to leave this to the editor and then blame him for mishaps, eg. if some of the reductions are too small or the plates are in the wrong order. The way to ensure the most effective production is to supervise the arrangement oneself. As photographs often have to be reproduced on special paper it is not always possible to have them placed opposite the text to which they refer. The editor and the printers must therefore work out a reasonable placing. If all the plates are to be put exactly where all contributors want them, it means that each plate has to be 'tipped in' or pasted into each volume individually at considerable expense. Far better to have them in groups, as in the *Journal of Roman Studies,* or distributed in the volume between the sheets of text.

Periodicals are printed on sheets of paper on both sides, and folded twice to produce eight sides (quarto) or three times to produce sixteen sides (octavo). When folded this appears as a run of four or eight pages in sequence in the text. The most economical method of adding plates is thus between these folded sheets of eight or sixteen sides, but it does not have to be in full sized sheets. If, for example, only two separate pages of plates are needed, quarto size, the sheet would be half the size of that of the text and folded once; if it is then placed so that eight pages of text (a full sheet) divide the two pages of plates, the latter will be bound into the volume, whereas the single pages cannot be thus incorporated and have to be pasted in by hand and more readily come adrift.

More and more books are being printed by offset lithography, which allows much greater flexibility in the placing of photographs, and societies are becoming more interested in this method on the grounds of economy.

Drawings of objects and pottery

In many reports published up to forty years ago it was the practice to illustrate pottery and small objects by photographs. But unless the quality of these is exceptional, it is far better and more economical to use drawings.

142

There are exceptions to this in the case of sculptured stone or particularly large objects or pieces of unusual artistic quality. The drawing of small objects presents a difficult problem to the beginner. Modest artistic gifts are needed and the drawings attempted by those without these talents or experience have a crude and clumsy appearance however accurate they may be. On the other hand, if an artist with no archaeological interest draws the objects they may be very finely executed but important details may be overlooked. There must be a very accurate observation of decoration and any functional parts. One should at least start by knowing what the object is and how it worked. There is a place here for amateurs who have talent and patience as well as interest and knowledge.[1]

The best results are usually obtained if the objects are drawn twice their actual size on good quality, smooth paper. A reduction by a half will then bring them down to the natural size for publication. All shading should be done as if the light source is at the top left-hand corner. Before embarking on this kind of enterprise one should study good-quality drawings of objects of different kinds of material. The Research Reports of the Society of Antiquaries and the British Museum Guides contain large numbers of excellent drawings of all types of objects and materials. There are ways of giving the effect of iron, bone, flint, glass and bronze by shading and stippling, as shown in the illustrated examples (figs. 18 and 19).

Prehistoric sites usually produce so few datable finds that the drawing of every scrap of pottery, worked stone and bone may be necessary. On Roman sites, however, there is so much material that some selection is clearly essential. It is doubtful if all the spindle-whorls, whetstones and bone pins should be presented as drawings, but if they are omitted in this form a note should appear, listing them and describing the materials of which they are made. Only in this way will a future student know that objects of this kind were found and can be studied further if necessary.

Pottery

Pottery sherds also need to be thoroughly sorted out, and the fragments selected for drawing should be only those which enable the site in general or a deposit in particular to be dated. There are exceptions to this rule. There may be, for example, the occasional sherd which is of interest in itself, or a site may produce an entirely new type of pottery which would need to be studied and as many sherds as possible published. Wasters and broken sherds from pottery kilns also require fuller treatment. There are

[1] A very useful introduction for the amateur is Conant Brodribb, *Drawing Archaeological Finds for Publication* (1970).

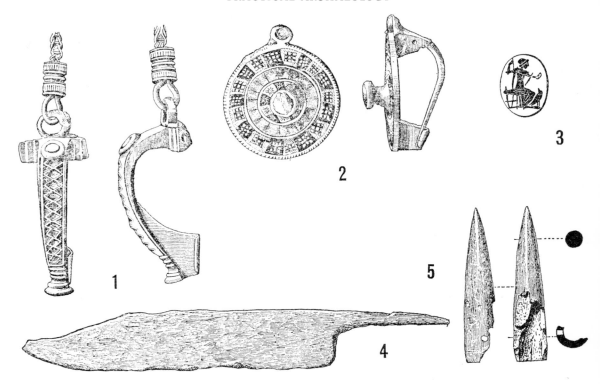

Fig. 18 Drawings of objects: 1 a bronze brooch ($\frac{1}{1}$); 2 an enamelled brooch ($\frac{1}{1}$); 3 an intaglio ($\frac{2}{1}$); 4 an iron knife ($\frac{1}{1}$); 5 a bone tool ($\frac{1}{2}$)

also sites which have been occupied for a short time only and produce a selection of contemporary types which could also be studied in more detail than usual. The first investigation of a site in an ill-explored region may also justify a wider selection—here even unstratified pottery might be included to show the main regional types and fabrics. Most late Iron Age, Roman and medieval excavations produce a great quantity of pottery and, once the initial selection has been decided, some sorting and discarding may be done on the site after the sherds have been washed. Later, the pottery is arranged in its stratified groups and a selection made of the vessels to be drawn for publication. The main factor influencing choice will be the characteristics helping to date the laying down of the deposit. As explained above (p. 55), on sites with a long period of occupation the later deposits will include much rubbish survival. Sherds from earlier levels should be rejected and only those which contribute to the dating of the deposit drawn. If this had been rigorously carried out in some earlier excavation

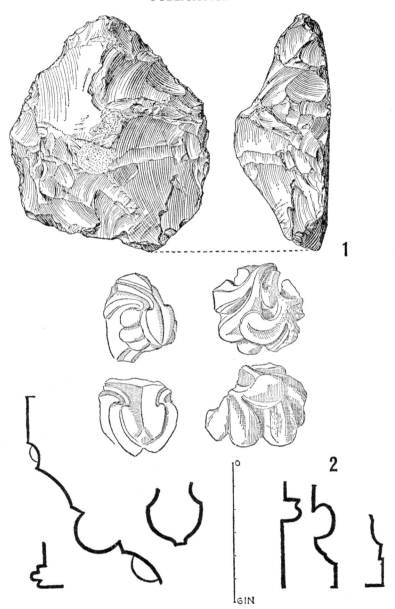

Fig. 19 Drawings of a flint object and stone mouldings: 1 a flint hand-axe ($\frac{1}{2}$); 2 examples of drawings and sections of stone mouldings.

145

reports there would have been considerably fewer drawings and less confusion for the beginner who tends to accept all the published groups as contemporary.

Some excavators prefer to classify all their sherds into types of fabric as recommended in *The Preparation of Archaeological Reports*. An example of this practice is seen in Dr K. Branigan's *Latimer* (1971). From this villa site 66 pottery types were isolated, including samian, and thereafter referred to by numbers. It is a system which has much to commend it where there are only a few types, as on an Iron Age site, but Romano-British pottery is far too varied to be treated in this way and it makes for difficulty in following the text. It is more important to maintain the stratified grouping and to try to identify the origins of the pottery.

The next stage in selection is to take away the sherds which are too small or fragmentary to illustrate but if, in spite of their size, they are datable by their fabric or decoration they must be mentioned in the text with the rest of the group. Normally the main dating characteristics are in the rim form, and body sherds and bases rarely contribute to knowledge. Care must however be taken to sort through the group and search for pieces of the same vessel which may help to determine its complete profile. Beginners tend to do this at the outset and then stick the pieces together in an attempt to build up the pot, but it may be difficult to draw the vessel in this condition so it is better merely to collect together all the sherds of the same vessel and mark the joins on the inner surface. Then when the drawing is done, pieces can be joined together as needed for completing the profile.

The standard method of drawing pottery is to show the section and internal surface on the left-hand side and the elevation with external surface on the right-hand side. The vessels are all drawn full size and, with certain exceptions, the block-maker's reduction is to a quarter. The exceptions to this reduction are either very large vessels where the reduction may be greater, or decoration, such as that on samian ware, where the reduction may be to a half. One should first select a pen with a suitable thickness.[1] Finer detail still, such as potters' stamps, may need to be reproduced at the same size and it is often better in these cases to draw the stamps double size.

Pottery is the commonest and most important class of small find and excavators have to acquire considerable knowledge of its varieties and dating characteristics as well as skill in drawing. For the latter one has no

---

[1] Such as a Rapidograph or Koh-i-Noor designer pen with a 0.6 mm stylus.

VIIIA   Drawing a piece of pottery.

VIIIB   Sorting out and marking pottery.

147

need for artistic ability—aptitude can be developed rapidly once the basic principles are appreciated. There are several methods of drawing pottery and complicated pieces of apparatus have even been devised to assist in this. Purely mechanical means, however, have their disadvantages as they rarely cause the person doing the drawing to examine the sherd as a piece of craftsmanship. For this reason it is far better to reduce the mechanical means to a minimum and draw as much as possible by eye. There is one basic measurement which is necessary at the outset—the rim diameter. This can be gauged very quickly on a rim scale whose arcs are drawn out in a series of radii: the rim is moved up and down until its curve fits one of them.

The drawing can be most easily done on graph-paper with a faint grey line which will not reproduce on the blockmaker's photograph. A horizontal line is chosen to represent the top of the vessel and the rim diameter set out and halved; at the centre a line is drawn at right-angles representing the division of the drawing into section and external elevation (fig. 21). Next, one takes the sherd in the left hand, resting the hand on the drawing board, and holds the sherd so that the rim is in the same horizontal plane as the diameter line drawn on the graph-paper. To help to determine this position one can use an engineer's square. This is a steel square with a heavy base and a piece which projects upwards at right-angles. The square is placed on the drawing so that the projecting part represents a vertical plane based on the horizontal drawn on the paper. The rim of the sherd is then placed against the square so that the plane of the rim, as it is held vertically on the paper, is coincident with the plane of the square (ph. VIIIA). At the same time the outermost point of the rim must be aligned to a point marked on the drawn diameter in such a way that when the eye is held immediately over this point the imaginary line from the eye to the graph-paper is tangential to the curve of the rim. If the sherd can be held firmly with the left hand in this position, the profile can be drawn direct with the right hand following the eye as it traces its tangential course round the rim and body of the vessel. After drawing the right-hand profile, it is advisable to turn the drawing upside down and repeat the process for the left-hand side. The two sides can then be checked against each other to ensure that the vessel has been held in the correct position. Having achieved symmetry, providing of course the vessel had been made on a wheel, the next tasks are to add the section and details of decoration. The section can be measured with calipers, but care must be exercised to make certain that a true thickness is drawn and a simpler and more accurate method may be that of direct measurement with a scale, holding the latter

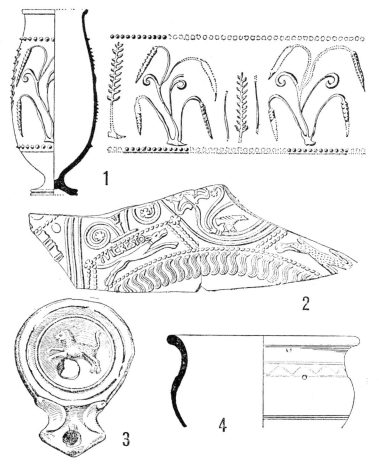

Fig. 20 Drawings of pottery: 1 a beaker with barbotine decoration ($\frac{1}{2}$); 2 a fragment of decorated samian ($\frac{1}{1}$); 3 a lamp ($\frac{1}{2}$); 4 a wide-mouth bowl ($\frac{1}{4}$).

always at right-angles to the body of the sherd and not along the plan of breakage. The surfaces of the vessel should be examined carefully for signs of decoration as these can often be very faint.

There are different ways of completing a drawing. The prehistorians prefer to show the vessel as it actually appears, and with careful shading and stippling portray the treatment and finish of the surface (figs. 20 and 21). To do this effectively some skill and artistry is needed.[1]

[1] Some of the finest examples of this type of drawing are those of Professor W. F. Grimes in *Excavations on Defence Sites, 1939-45* (H M S O 1960).

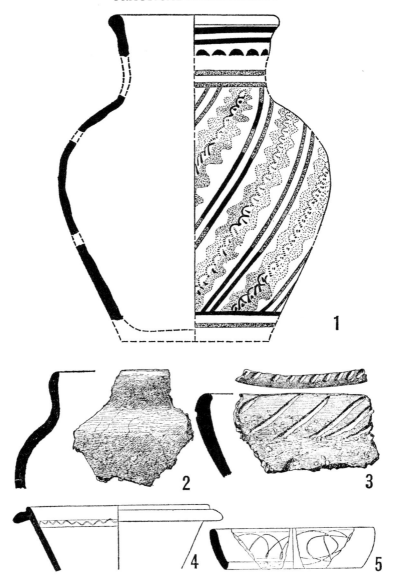

Fig. 21 Drawings of pottery: 1 a medieval jug with polychrome decoration ($\frac{1}{2}$); 2 and 3 Iron Age pottery ($\frac{1}{2}$); 4 a Romano-British bead and flanged bowl ($\frac{1}{4}$); 5 a black-burnished bowl with incised decoration ($\frac{1}{4}$).

The same methods could be applied to the pottery of all other periods and some have attempted this from the days of Pitt-Rivers who employed a staff of skilled artists and draughtsmen. Faced, however, with the great bulk of Romano-British material, excavators have quailed before the immense labour involved and have shown only the positive elements of decoration. There is undoubtedly a problem here in the case of vessels which have received some form of surface treatment, such as polishing or burnishing, and it would seem desirable to attempt to show these effects. Whether the work entailed in this is commensurate with the results to be achieved is a question not easily resolved. It is largely a matter of time and ability and this must be a personal decision. The medieval excavators also face this problem with the vessels which have been knife-trimmed and the tendency here seems to be a compromise in which there is an indication rather than a completely realistic portrayal of the surface treatment. It may be necessary on occasion to illustrate vessels with photographs which show their appearance more effectively than drawings and description. This practice must be limited to new or unusual types. Publication can never really convey the essential characteristics of a ware, and archaeologists should try to handle pottery as much as possible before accepting similarities on the basis of illustration.

Once the drawings have all been traced or mounted on a sheet for the block-makers they can be numbered serially. Now the problem arises of listing all the sherds with adequate descriptions. An attempt has been made in the *CBA Research Report no. 6.*[1] to put this into a simple but consistent order, ie. 1. class or type of vessel; 2. details of form and condition where significant; 3. fabric; 4. decoration. The Guide itself lists most of the types of vessels found on Romano-British sites and gives names to them together with notes on particular wares and manufacturing techniques. Two real difficulties are in giving precise definitions of fabric and colour. The terms 'sandy', 'gritty' or 'hard' are entirely subjective, but until someone prepares a chart based perhaps on a sequence of graduated sand-papers, the fabric descriptions will remain vague and unsatisfactory. The problem of colour is also difficult. There are colour charts which can be used[2] but the surfaces of vessels often vary very greatly in colour a condition due

[1] *Romano-British Coarse Pottery: A Students Guide* (2nd edn 1969).
[2] Such as the Munsell system; a colour-chart has been prepared by the Study Group for Romano-British pottery (obtainable from Rescue, 5a The Tything, Worcester, £1.50).

to the position of the pot in the kiln. Colour changes are caused if the vessel has been used for cooking, and sub-soil conditions can also affect the surface in some cases by removing it altogether. It is possible to find fitting sherds with totally different colours. For example, a black burnished cooking pot which is normally dense black in colour will become bright red when fired in an open hearth and cooled under oxidising conditions. One should therefore use colour charts with a great deal of discretion, but it might at least prevent the same vessel being described by different observers as buff, orange, red or light brown.

It is important that somewhere in the report there should be a note as to where the finds have been deposited so that future students can see and handle them.

Proofs

When an editor has received enough material for his transactions, he will send it along to the printers. Twelve months usually elapse between the receipt of the manuscripts and the delivery of the printed volume. The printer supplies the editor with proofs at two stages, in galley and page form. The galleys are long strips of text before it has been divided up into individual pages, all the footnotes appearing together at the end. The editor should send these galleys to the contributors for checking and with them will be the printed samples taken from the line and half-tone blocks—these are called pulls. The latter may be very rough indeed and must not be taken as an indication of the appearance of the final version. The text must be checked through very carefully and if possible counter-checked by someone else not familiar with it. Since the typescript should always be the final version, the only alterations, apart from author's mistakes, should be the correction of typographical errors. It seems very simple to start adding and deleting words and phrases to improve the text, but this can be a very expensive business as it takes time and skill to alter the type.[1] Nowadays it is becoming customary for editors to send contributors a bill for the cost of these alterations if they are excessive, and the over-zealous writer may find that his improvements cost him several pounds. It is thus essential that the typescript should be complete in detail with correct punctuation, paragraphing and headings; then there will be no need to start reshaping the galleys.

If it is essential to make an alteration, care should be taken to see that the number of letters and spaces inserted is the same as that taken out. The

---

[1] It costs 25p to change a comma to a full-stop.

printer will then be able to localise the alteration, and not have to shunt his type from one line to another to make up the space. Archaeologists, and anyone else seeking to publish, ought to visit a printing works to see exactly how type is set up. They would then appreciate the problems involved in even minor amendments, and would not treat checking of the galleys as an occasion for redrafting.[1] Proof corrections have been standardised and a table of symbols can be obtained.[2] These should be carefully followed if the author's intentions are to be made clear to the printer. After the correction and return of the galley proofs, the contributor does not normally see his work until it appears in its published form. Page proofs are usually corrected by the editor in order to save time and to prevent any further alterations a contributor might be tempted to make.

As indicated above, it is difficult to alter blocks once they are made except to remove words or lines on a line block. The pulls are sent to contributors so that they can check the captions. It is not possible at this stage to insert the numbers of the plates and figures either on the pulls or in the text as they will not be known until the whole volume is in page form and the numbering sequence finalised. These blanks will be filled in later by the editor.

At proof stage the contributor can tell the editor how many offprints he is likely to need. It is customary in most societies to allow each contributor a free issue of twelve or more offprints, but these will not cover his needs if those who have given help and advice and all his volunteers are to be given copies, so additional ones are ordered which will have to be paid for by the contributor, although the cost is usually fairly modest.

Conclusion

In this brief survey an attempt has been made to describe the processes of archaeological enquiry from the discovery of a site to the production of a published report. During these stages, lasting in most cases some years, the archaeologist needs to acquire an all-round discipline, neglecting no detail at any point, and developing his techniques to full efficiency. There is, however, always a serious danger of these techniques becoming an end in themselves and in the effort to achieve perfection in their execution the

[1] A useful little pamphlet on these problems, *Author's alterations cost money and cause delay,* can be obtained from the British Federation of Master Printers, 11 Bedford Row, London WC1. See also *Preparation of Manuscripts and Correction of Proofs,* 1951, and H. Hart, *Rules for Compositors and Readers.*

[2] *Table of Symbols for Printers' and Authors' Proof Corrections,* British Standard Institute, no. 1219C (1958).

greater need for full interpretation may be overlooked. A site may be skilfully excavated but no knowledge gained of the people who lived there. The most difficult art, which some may never acquire, is that of interpreting the excavation as phases of human activity. This is the sole purpose of the enquiry, to see how men lived and died at a certain moment of time. In doing this the archaeologist may come to a closer understanding of Man himself and even share this experience with a wider audience.

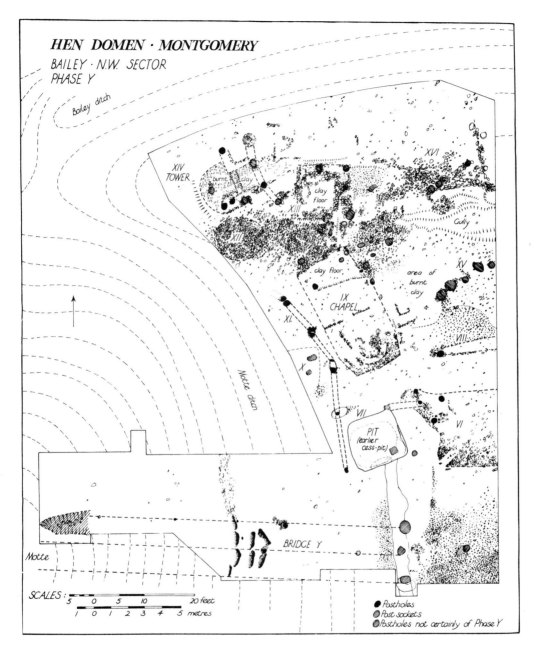

Figure 22
Plan of Hen Domen, Montgomeryshire

Index

Abney
   clinometer, 39
Actus, 25
Aerial photography, 45, Fig. I; type of camera, 46; reconnaissance, 40–46
Agriculture, 22–26; implements of, 23–24; evidence for—beneath barrows, 24 (fn), 61–62.
Aitken, M.J., 49 (fn), 50, 114 (fn)
Alcester, Warwickshire, 110
Alexander, H., 19 (fn)
America, archaeology in, 114, 119
Amlwch, Parys Mountain, Anglesey, copper workings at, 34
Ancient Fields, 23
Ancient Peoples and Places Series, *see* Thames and Hudson
Anglesey, 34; R.C.H.M. volume, II, 26 (fn)
Anglo-Saxon, *see* Saxon
Annual Report of the C.B.A., *see* C.B.A.
Antiquaries of London, Society of, 12, *Antiquaries Journal*, 12, 130; *Archaeologia*, 12; *Proceedings*, 12; Research Reports, 13, 143
Antiquaries of Scotland, Society of, 14, *Proceedings of*, 14
Antiquaries Journal, The, *see* Antiquaries of London, Society of
Antiquity, 14
Antonine Wall, 28
'Antonius', Emperor, 17
Archaeologia, *see*, Antiquaries of London, Society of
Archaeologia Cambrensis, *see* Cambrian Association
Archaeological Journal, *see* Royal Archaeological Institute

Archaeology of the Cambridge Region, 10
Archaeometry, 51 (fn)
Arkell, W.S., 109 (fn)
Ashbee, Paul, 30 (fn)
Atkinson, R.J.C., 38 (fn), 47
Avebury, 8

Bailey, motte and, 29
Baginton, near Coventry, 74 (fn)
Banks, *see* ramparts
Barker, Philip, 29 (fn), 78, 82, 92 (fn)
Barnack, Northants, medieval quarries at, 37
Barnsley Park, Roman Villa, field system at, 24
Barrows: Bronze Age, 24 (fn), 53; excavation of, by quadrant method, 61–62, Fig. 2; long—, excavation of, 62–63; place-name, 17–18; Roman, 30; recognition of 30–31
Barton, K.J., 118 (fn)
Bath, 28
Bath-stone, use of, 109
Baulks, 82
Belshé, J.C., 115 (fn)
Benzotrizole, use of in treating bronze, 108
Beorg, place-name, 18
Beresford, M.W., 26 (fn), 29 (fn), 80 (fn)
Berm, Fig. 7
Berrow, place-name, 18
Bersu, Professor, 80, 136
Beveridge, W.I.B., 100 (fn)
Bibliography, Annual, *see* C.B.A.
Biddle, Martin, 78, 96 (fn)
Birchall, Ann, 116 (fn)
Birmingham, University of, 5
Blake, Bryan, 118 (fn)
'Bleeper', 50
Blin-Stoyle, A.E., 112 (fn)
Blocks, 153; half tone, 141; line, 133

157